POETRY EMOTIONS

The Joys Of Life

Edited by Jenni Bannister

First published in Great Britain in 2016 by:

Young Writers

Remus House
Coltsfoot Drive
Peterborough
PE2 9BF
Telephone: 01733 890066
Website: www.youngwriters.co.uk
All Rights Reserved
Book Design by Ashley Janson
© Copyright Contributors 2016
SB ISBN 978-1-78624-229-7

Printed and bound in the UK by BookPrintingUK
Website: www.bookprintinguk.com

Foreword

Welcome, Reader!

For Young Writers' latest competition, *Poetry Emotions*, we gave school children nationwide the task of writing a poem all about emotions, and they rose to the challenge magnificently!

Pupils could either write about emotions they've felt themselves or create a character to represent an emotion. Which one they chose was entirely up them. Our aspiring poets have also developed their creative skills along the way, getting to grips with poetic techniques such as rhyme, simile and alliteration to bring their thoughts to life. The result is this entertaining collection that allows us a fascinating glimpse into the minds of the next generation, giving us an insight into their innermost feelings. It also makes a great keepsake for years to come.

Here at Young Writers our aim is to encourage creativity in children and to inspire a love of the written word, so it's great to get such an amazing response, with some absolutely fantastic poems. This made it a tough challenge to pick the winners, so well done to *Craig Tyrrell* who has been chosen as the best author in this anthology.

I'd like to congratulate all the young authors in *Poetry Emotions – The Joys Of Life* – I hope this inspires them to continue with their creative writing.

Editorial Manager

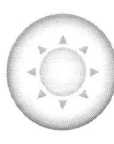

Our charity partner for this academic year is . . .

YOUNGMINDS
The voice for young people's **mental health and wellbeing**

We're aiming to raise a huge £5,000 this academic year to help raise awareness for YoungMinds and the great work they do to support children and young people.

If you would like to get involved visit
www.justgiving.com/Young-Writers

YoungMinds is the UK's leading charity committed to improving the emotional wellbeing and mental health of children and young people. They campaign, research and influence policy and practice on behalf of children and young people to improve care and services. They also provide expert knowledge to professionals, parents and young people through the Parents' Helpline, online resources, training and development, outreach work and publications. Their mission is to improve the emotional resilience of all children and to ensure that those who suffer ill mental health get fast and effective support.

www.youngminds.org.uk

Contents

Arisa Gohar (9) 1
Oumou Kesso Barry (11) 2
Drishti Goel (12) 3
James Inglis (10) 3
Grace Clare Godwin (9) 4
Shema Byrne (7) 4
Vishal Mann (10) 5
Amy Chisem (9) 5
Matthew Sargeant (8) 6
April-Grace Levell (8) 6
Lucy Parsons (10) 7
Reece Ray (8) 7

Ashdale Care Ltd, Ballygawley

Rachel Stewart (11) 8
Craig Tyrrell 8

Brentfield Primary School, London

Symika Smartt (9) 9
Salma Hashi (9) 9
Abdulla Nasir (9) 10
Rayhan Pawes (10) 10
Abdirixman Mohamed (10) 11
Majid Farah (10) 11
Shubham Madhu (9) 12
Inaas Ali (9) 12
Tyreal (9) 13

Brookfield Special School, Craigavon

Sam Toner (9) 13
Odhrán Magennis (9) 14
Kai Naylor (10) 14
Rylan Boyd (10) 14
Cormác James O'Connor (10) 15
Tiernan Munce (10) 15
Shea Nesbitt (9) 15
Nathan Tabb (9) 16

Bushvalley Primary School, Ballymoney

Patrick James Harrison (10) 16
Simon Lavery (11) 17
Stacey Louise King (11) 17
Laura Stewart (10) 18
Mia McConaghie (11) 18
Ben Russell Robinson (11) 19
Johnny Huey (10) 19
Emma McAfee (10) 20
Elisha Van Der Byl (10) 20
Abigail Jane Sayers (10) 21
Mark Chestnutt (11) 21
Erin Armstrong (10) 22
Adam James Feeney (10) 22
Kurt Wright (11) 23
Paula Lamont (11) 23
Jill Stirling (10) 24
Brian Patton (10) 24
Callum Gibson (11) 25
Alex Christie (11) 25
Ellie McFadden (11) 26
Bailey Ayres (10) 26
Matthew Craig (10) 26

Cedars Park Primary School, Stowmarket

Georgia Moore (11) 27
Millie Bayes (11) 28
Lily Ruscoe (11) 29
Jack Atkins (10) 30
Kenzie Springall (11) 31
Paulina Latka (11) 32
Toby Isaacs 32
Molly Mayhew (10) 33
Savannah Cross (10) 33
Jessica Terrell (10) 34
Morgan Cansdale (11) 35
Emma Balaam (11) 36
Elizabeth Elmer (10) 36

Ellie Ames (10) 37
Harry Coffey (11) 37
Kody Thomas (11) 38
Louise Blair (11) 39
Rosie Ager (11) 40
Kate Marie Chapman (10) 40
Kian Patel (10) 41
Chloe Leeder (10) 41
Mia Turner (11) 42
Alexander Crawford (10) 42
Amelia Elizabeth Fokinther (11) 43
Luke Beamish (10) 43
Hannah May Chevin (11) 44
Tara King (11) 44
Sophie Norris (11) 45
Eloise Jackson (10) 45
Finley Davis (10) 46
Jack Webb (10) 46

Charlton Primary School, Wantage
Ella Thompson (10) 47
Joseph Quinan (10) 47
Olivia Moor (9) 47
Jolie Camden (8) 48

Divine Saviour RC Primary School, Abbots Langley
Harry Reeves (9) 48

Elmlea Junior School, Bristol
Jeffery Guo (8) 48
Evan Baker (10) 49
Joe Preddy (9) 50
Rose O'Brien (8) 51
Eloise Allen (9) 52
Ben Mcilree 53
John Suggett 53
Suki Linstead (8) 54
Mani Cresswell (8) 54
Alex Peter Morris (9) 55
Anna Mahon (10) 56
Alex Davidson (8) 56
Lucy Ashworth 57
Zoey Yan Starke (10) 57
Emily Inch 58
Lucy Regan (10) 58
Sebastian (8) 59

Sam Bristow (8) 59
Lottie Lewis (10) 60

Gatten And Lake Primary School, Shanklin
Ellis Robson (11) 60
Molly Faithfull 61
Molly Bennett 62
Caitlin Dologhan (9) 63
Madison Lexi Collins (8) 63
Maddison Kim Elizabeth Harrop (10) 64
Lauren Brooke Riordan Moore (10) 64
Charlie Cule (8) 65
Tegan Leigh Brown (9) 65
Fraser Lloyd (8) 66
Lewis Brand 66
Jessica Jayne Cooper (9) 67
Bobby Curtis (9) 67
Leon Philips King (11) 68
Caitlin Birtwistle (8) 68
Amber-Rae Adkins-Hughes (10) 69
Benjamin Mark Moralee (8) 69
Kubra Nur Korkmaz (10) 70
George Hayward (11) 70
Ruby Bodenham 71
Aaron Cooper 71
Abigail Marie Bird 72
Charlie Crabb 72
Alicia Davison 73
Ellie Mai Potts (10) 73
Aiden Dumbleton (10) 74
Harry William Byron (10) 74
Lauren Acons 74
Jess Beckley (10) 75
James Ashley 75
Doman Madaras 75
Kaymen Lee Freddie Cooch (8) 76
Harvey P 76
Leio Alexander Mellanby-Smith (6) 76
Sophie Frewing (10) 77
Mason Damien Jupe 77
Amari Tafari Ralston Blake (10) 77
Harrison Abbott (7) 78
Ava Guy 78
Logan Shields 78
Ruby-May Bristow 79
Lennix James Mellanby-Smith (9) 79

Ruby Ridgway-Bamford 79
Evie Thomas 80
Ellie Russel (11) 80
Toby Page (8) 81
Harrison James Chapman (10) 81

International School Of Gabon, Libreville
Ridhi Singhagra (7) 82
Alastair Issei Ruark (7) 82
Jeremy Kei Ruark (7) 83
Hannah Bruce (8) 83

Iqra Slough Islamic Primary School, Slough
Mishal Baig (8) 84
Nusayba Yusuf (8) 85
M Fosi (9) 86

Jumeirah English Speaking School, Dubai
Anika Jethwani 86
Aryav J. Odhrani (8) 87
Dasuni Gunasekara (8) 88
Kiara Dhamecha (8) 89
Kiana Sathyanarayanan (8) 90
Ishana Khiara (8) 91
Rebecca Bainbridge (7) 92
Rania Jethwani (8) 92

Katesgrove Primary School, Reading
Adam Kovalev Brown (11) 93
Akshay Tumunuri (11) 94
Laiba Shafiq (10) 95
Ayusha Shakya (11) 96
Maizie Rae Townsend (11) 97
Reem Abdulmagied (11) 98
Shubham Kulkarni (11) 99
Mehar Bhatia (11) 100

Kilmodan Primary School, Colintraive
Sinead Kennedy 100
Hugo Charles Leigh (8) 101
Jadelouise Madeline Robertson (8) 102

Newbuildings Primary School, Londonderry
Anna Campbell 102
George Guy 103
Dayne Roberts 103
Rebekah Loughlin (10) 104
Ella Hughes (10) 104
Ellie Byron 105
Abbie Thompson 105
Alex Campbell 106
Rachel Watson 106

Oak Field Primary School, Barry
Ella Leanne Phillips (9) 107
Charleigh-Kate Wheatley (11) 107
Leo Phillips (10) 108
Gabriella Robson 108
Malachi Mattraves (8) 109
Brooke Leigh Seer (10) 109
Chantelle Wheatley 109
Kairan Cummins-Free (8) 110
Ellis Miller (8) 110
Maddison Brady 110

Plasnewydd Primary School, Maesteg
Kadee Leigh Williams 111
Lucy Marie Davies (11) 111
Ethan Lloyd Morris (11) 112
Lucie Daniel (10) 112
Rebecca Leigh Jones (10) 113
Ethan Saxby 113
Harvey Ellis Williams 114
Sam Powell 114
Lily May Lavercombe (11) 115
Lola Olivia Videan (11) 115
Katie Louise Thomas (10) 116
Ethan Morgan Seymour (11) 116
Hayden Smith 117
Macie Freeman 117
India Williams 118
Ellie Mullins 118
Nieve Keddy 119
Casey White 119

Natisha Blower 120
Ffion Rumph (11) 120
Olivia Castle 121
Charlie Acteson 121

Platt CE Primary School, Sevenoaks
Leah Grevatt (10) 122
Bryer Icela Zagas Lowe (7) 123

Stepping Stones School, Hindhead
Georgia Ellen Stronge (15) 124
Hannah (Bo) Longley 125
Jade Lily Mansell (15) 126
Lucas Harman 126

Talmud Torah Tiferes Shlomoh, London
Yisrolik Itzinger (10) 127
Refoel Duvid Weitz (11) 127
Moishy Fierstone 128
Boruch Freshwater 128
Shmelky Pinter (10) 129

The Poems

POETRY EMOTIONS - The Joys Of Life

Roller Coaster Of Emotions

I can't believe I'm doing this,
What a scary thought;
It's an opportunity I just can't miss!

As I look up at the daunting structure of twisted metal
I feel butterflies in my tummy;
And my head feels light as a petal.

I reluctantly, yet excitedly edge forward to a seat,
Feeling a shot of joy, I lower the safety pole;
I lay back feeling sweaty, hoping I can stand the heat.

As the humming begins, I feel a tingle in my toes,
I think, *This is fine, I can handle this*
Suddenly, with a *whoosh!* off it goes.

Ascending the steep metal tower
There I feel small droplets of water;
On the descent, that's when I really feel the power!

Kerplosh! As it rises over my head, the cool mist settles on my face,
I wish I could capture this moment in a jar;
But all memories will fade away just like a
winner in a race.

As the log turns a corner there is a bright flash,
A photo has been taken of my soaked self;
The ride is coming to an end with an almighty splash!

The end of the ride makes me feel low,
But wait! There's the line;
I'll join it again and have another go!

Arisa Gohar (9)

Goodbye Best Friend

Goodbye my best friend and take care!

For all these years we have been friends,
Loving you until the end.
For all the cheer that we have shared,
Tenderly loving you until the end.
For all these months and all these years
Loving you until the end.

When friendship comes first
And this which will never burst,
The lines that we have reached
So remember me when I'm gone.

I feel like i just met you and now you move away
And I very shyly know that this is your last day
I pray we will keep in touch, I pray because of the past
I'd say those things and promise stuff but they don't seem to last.

When I go please don't be sad,
Even though I might be a little mad.
I'm always gonna love you until the end,
I really hope to see you again.

You're the first friend I have met and I cherish you a bunch
And although our time may have been short, know I love you very much!

Oumou Kesso Barry (11)

POETRY EMOTIONS - The Joys Of Life

Tears

Under the extreme guidance of emotions,
They live together in our eyes.
They always flow,
When our emotions overflow,
They come out in happiness,
They come out in sadness.
So for the next time when they flow from your eyes,
Say to them everything is fine,
Tell them not to come again,
Because the situation will always be the same
And if they roll over from your eyes in happiness,
Let them spread.
But be calm at that time and remember,
'Change is the unchanging law of life'.

Drishti Goel (12)

Angry And Bored

A m I the only one that feels like this?
N ot knowing when I can play the games I miss
G etting rid of my console is wrong
R ight now the emotions I feel are strong
Y ou frustrate me and drive me crazy

A s well as being angry
N ever to be happy
D o you really have to punish me?

B y the way, my parents arc right
O n the days I listen to them, things are bright
R est assured I will play again
E arning my rewards now and then
D elighted to play, I am happy again!

James Inglis (10)

GG Poem

C rying is not happy
H appy is made when you get new football boots
R hyming is sometimes happiness but not all the time
I nside me there's this small gap, can I have a bit of happiness? Will it come back?
S mall gaps are good for happiness but not all the time
T eachers sometimes make me feel happy by the things they say
M ums make you feel happy
A crostic poems might
S anta makes me feel happy, not just because he gives me presents.

Grace Clare Godwin (9)

Open Day

Open day is tomorrow at school
Will my work go on display?
Maybe, maybe not!
No one knows
Could it be possible?
Maybe I should not even go at all
Maybe I should shout
Maybe I should stutter
I am so scared about open day
If my work is not on display
My mum will ground me for a year
Then will fall a hurtful tear.

Shema Byrne (7)

POETRY EMOTIONS - The Joys Of Life

Birthday Here

It's your birthday here,
So don't shed a tear,
I've got something for you to hear,
As it is your special year.

Have fun,
While you play with everyone,
Play friendly
And pray kindly.

Have a great day,
You will have your way
But remember, you have to pay.

Vishal Mann (10)

The Things That Scare Me At Night

When I go to bed at night
These are the things that give me a fright,
Hairy spiders ever so black,
Red-handed burglars filling up their sacks,
Murderers running on the go,
They're coming towards me, 'Oh no!'
Roaring tigers and their deathly bite,
These are the things that scare me at night.

Amy Chisem (9)

Happy

I felt happy when I scored my 100th goal
of the season.
I feel as happy as a dog barking
Because I just came back from holiday.

I feel happy when I'm with my friends.
I feel as happy as a fish who felt safe from the giant blue whale.

I feel happy when I eat chocolate cake.
I feel as happy as a dolphin laughing
When it's with its friends.

Matthew Sargeant (8)

Happy Days

I woke up seeing the hot, blazing sun shining
It's summertime!
Let's go swimming in the sea
And build brilliant castles in the sand
I'm extremely excited
I'm seeing my friends soon
And merrily meeting Mum at McDonald's
What a delightful day.

April-Grace Levell (8)

POETRY EMOTIONS - The Joys Of Life

My Love Message

Mom, we love you so,
You have a lovely warm glow.
You've been great to me and my sister
And even kind to the mister!
You put your back into everything,
Washing and every meal.
So in this poem we seal
Our undying love for you.

Lucy Parsons (10)

Emotions Poem

Emotions, emotions, emotions
Are what you feel
You feel angry, excited, sad, happy
They're all emotions.

Reece Ray (8)

Untitled

I love swimming in the sea
We are as busy as buzzy bees
Brrr . . . it's really cold
I wrap up warm as good as gold

I love eating fish and chips
When I'm finished I smack my lips
I enjoy tasty mint chocolate chip ice cream
With a flake and strawberry sauce it's fit for a queen

The funfair is noisy and big
On the beach we play tig
I love speeding on the bumper cars
I could enjoy them for hours and hours

Rachel Stewart (11)
Ashdale Care Ltd, Ballygawley

Why I Love My Country

I love my country although it rains,
I go inside to watch the Gaelic games.
My country is famous for its brew,
Grab a bowl of steaming stew.

Ireland is called the Emerald Isle,
We have our own dance in a traditional style.
Come and listen to an Irish legend,
About Finn McCool and his mighty weapon.

We are a proud country in all we do,
We have lots of landmarks with a great view.
Ireland is a lucky land,
So come to Ireland and all will be grand.

Craig Tyrrell
Ashdale Care Ltd, Ballygawley

POETRY EMOTIONS - The Joys Of Life

My Confident Monster

I am feeling confident
Like I can do anything.
When you feel confident
You can do many things.

I think I need to scream!
It's bubbling up my throat.
My confident monster is going to burst
And soon you will know.

I'm confident that I'll win,
Because I've won before you see.
And if people want any ideas
Then I think they should follow me.

Here comes my scream,
I think I should go.
'Argh!'
I told you you would know!

Symika Smartt (9)
Brentfield Primary School, London

The Silver Bullet

Angry lives in the deepest part where nightmares are.
It comes out when you make it.
It will make you a different person that you will never want to be.
Anger is really bad.
It goes when you hug it
And it will disappear for days.
Everyone will run away and never come back again.
Be careful not to get someone angry
'Cause it will be the worst day of your life.
Anger is horrible.
Anger is bad.
Anger is the worst emotion.

Salma Hashi (9)
Brentfield Primary School, London

What I Did To My Brother

Once I kicked my brother,
He called out for our mother.
She was very angry,
So I didn't have any candy.

I stamped on the stairs,
I knocked down the chairs.
I was very mad,
I became bad.

I was very sorry,
Then came my friend Corey.
We played outside
And it was good weather.

I know what I did wrong.
I was angry for too long!
But now I'm filled with joy
Because my mum bought me a toy.

Abdulla Nasir (9)
Brentfield Primary School, London

The Evil Anger

As fierce as a lion he jumps out,
He is ready to shout.
He is your evil emotion,
So put on some lotion
To cool the angry flames down
Or have a scary frown.
He has a burning crown.
Watch out for his aggressive attack,
Your friends will be flocking back.
If your anger is running fast,
Be sure to take an anger management class.

Rayhan Pawes (10)
Brentfield Primary School, London

POETRY EMOTIONS - The Joys Of Life

Anger

Solve it with your warm hugs,
Just don't make a fuss.
We all have something to fear
So have a great cheer.
But it's trying to fight back.
It's really got an act.
Fearful as a scare,
As big as my hair.
At the top of my voice I scream,
What is anger?
it is an emotion that can take you over
Not a four leaf clover.
But anger is a strong emotion,
Punch a pillow.
I hug my pet willow.
Help yourself with some ice cream.
Calm down and break free nicely.

Abdirixman Mohamed (10)
Brentfield Primary School, London

My Birthday

H appiness is the way I feel on my birthday
A nd for friends and family
P laying together
P lanning something special for me
I 'm ten today
N o bad weather is here today
E veryone came to my house
S ay happy birthday
S o happy!

Majid Farah (10)
Brentfield Primary School, London

Angriness!

They teased me,
They hated me.

I grew spikes
Just like knives.

They laughed,
They clapped,
They had a big laugh.

I thudded and I huffed and I puffed,
I nearly blew the away
But they never listened.

Suddenly rain came down
And all my anger was gone
And we started playing.

Shubham Madhu (9)
Brentfield Primary School, London

Sadness

I feel so alone and sad up that tree,
'Cause no one comes to play with me.
I get bullied every single day
Does anyone want to play?
No.
Anger just came out, joy died out
I have no pride, I have no life,
I can't survive
Without pride and happiness in my life.
I am Sadness, what can I do?
I'd rather curl up in a corner
And cry till the moon comes down
And the sun flies away.

Inaas Ali (9)
Brentfield Primary School, London

POETRY EMOTIONS - The Joys Of Life

Untitled

When I am happy,
I hang upside down.
My smile turns upside down,
But maybe it's a frown.

Tyreal (9)
Brentfield Primary School, London

Sad Sam

I was disappointed today because,
William didn't come to play,
He wanted to play with my toys and the other boys.

William is my cousin and he likes to play Minecraft,
He likes to splash on rafts.

He sometimes plays tag,
He usually builds cool stuff,
He sometimes goes on the laptop,
He plays outside,
He sometimes goes on the trampoline!

That's my favourite!

Sam Toner (9)
Brookfield Special School, Craigavon

Christmas Poem

C hristmas is a fun day
H appy, happy, I am feeling today
R unning around in the snow
I must not fall, oh no!
S anta is here today
T he toys are cool
M e and my friends play with the toys
A fun day for me
S anta says, 'Merry Christmas!'

Odhrán Magennis (9)
Brookfield Special School, Craigavon

Happiness

Happiness is a bright rainbow
The taste of happiness is fresh crunchy apples
Happiness is the smell of fresh flowers on the grass
It sounds like laughing kids
Happiness is joy from the inside

Kai Naylor (10)
Brookfield Special School, Craigavon

Happiness

Happiness is fun
The taste of ripe strawberries and cream
Happiness smells of Lynx Africa
It sounds like love
Happiness is laughter

Rylan Boyd (10)
Brookfield Special School, Craigavon

POETRY EMOTIONS - The Joys Of Life

Happiness

Happiness is all of my friends playing
And the taste of fresh bananas.
Happiness is the smell of my dog getting out of the bath;
It sounds like my dog's playful bark while I'm playing with her.
Happiness is the most important thing in life.

Cormác James O'Connor (10)
Brookfield Special School, Craigavon

Happiness

Happiness is my friends
That taste of Starbucks caramel hot chocolate
Happiness is the smell of freedom
It sounds like my wee baby nephew saying, 'Baba!'
Happiness is my friends

Tiernan Munce (10)
Brookfield Special School, Craigavon

Love

Love looks like a warm hug
Love sounds like happiness
Love feels like a giant hug
Love tastes like chocolates
Love smells like flowers

Shea Nesbitt (9)
Brookfield Special School, Craigavon

Love

Love looks like playing the Xbox
Love sounds like Minecraft
Love feels like holding the Xbox controller
Love tastes like chocolate

Nathan Tabb (9)
Brookfield Special School, Craigavon

Jealousy

Jealousy lives in a gloomy corner
She likes the dark and hates the bright
Jealousy is unseen, then she pounces
Then she waits and waits day and night.

Jealousy lives in a grey rainstorm
She will always say yes to a good pout
Jealousy is a squirming worm of spite
Where no one can pull you out.

Someone with a brand-new bike
It's a lot of tempting food
Jealousy has a big appetite
And won't hesitate to put you in a mood.

Jealousy please play with us
Please don't be a sin
No matter how hard you try
She refuses to join in.

Patrick James Harrison (10)
Bushvalley Primary School, Ballymoney

POETRY EMOTIONS - The Joys Of Life

Joy

She feels like lying on
A nice warm beach,
She lives in your heart
Like a never-ending ice cream sundae.
She feels like running through clouds,
Tastes like gooey, hot, creamy marshmallows.
Joy is yellow like the sun,
A wishing star,
Whizzing over your head.
She distrusts anger because he
Is a raging inferno.
She dislikes envy because once she
Starts she will never stop.
Joy is friendship and excitement because
They go together like a cat and a kitten.

Joy, joy, joy.

Simon Lavery (11)
Bushvalley Primary School, Ballymoney

Joy

I'm Joy.
I'm not a boy.
I'm the smile in your heart.
I'm the joke that makes you laugh.

I'm Joy.
I'm the sun in the sky,
The soft yellow light
That shines in your eyes.

I'm like a great new world.
I'm the best emotion
You can feel.
I'm Joy.

Stacey Louise King (11)
Bushvalley Primary School, Ballymoney

True Happiness

Happiness lies not
In wearing the latest, funky trends,
Nor is it being popular
And having many friends.
It cannot be purchased,
It's not wrapped up in a bow,
It's not all in certificates
Nailed up on the wall in show.
You can't attach a value,
It's priceless beyond compare -
Yet everyone can afford it
And it won't diminish if you share.
So what is this special treasure
That sets us apart from all the rest?
True happiness is the love and faith
That resides inside your chest.

Laura Stewart (10)
Bushvalley Primary School, Ballymoney

Wilma Worry

Oh Wilma Worry, why are you so sad?
You can make other people go rather mad!
Way deep down in our hearts you hide
Then sometimes you pounce and come outside!

When you walk along with me
My happiness you kill
And sometimes you linger far too long
Making a mountain out of a molehill.

It's time to shake you off, my friend
So I've shared you with my brother.
I'm too young to feel this way
So save it 'til I'm older!

Mia McConaghie (11)
Bushvalley Primary School, Ballymoney

Pleasure Is Here

Pleasure comes out on a summer's day,
When Pleasure comes out, she's ready to play.
Pleasure leisurely looks up in the sky
While slowly devouring a custard cream pie.
Skipping, whistling and even winning,
Smiling, running and singing
Are all the things that Pleasure likes to do -
Watch me, and pleasure you're sure to feel too!

Summer's here and school's out
Which means Pleasure's about!
Pleasure lives deep, deep down when
summer's around.
Pleasure looks like the burning yellow sun,
Jumping and dancing,
Primed for fun!

Ben Russell Robinson (11)
Bushvalley Primary School, Ballymoney

Happiness

She likes to cheer people up,
She'll always come out when you're
having a good time,
Sometimes you expect her, sometimes not.

She has a best friend she calls Joy who helps her
Fight your anger and sadness
And she does it well, with all her might.

She's like a smooth sandy beach
With a clear blue sky,
A power that scares Anger and Sadness far away.

She's found in a joyful, cosy home
Where no horrible emotion is welcome.
She is Happiness.

Johnny Huey (10)
Bushvalley Primary School, Ballymoney

My Envy

It lies in the shadows deep underground,
In a part of the earth where there is no sound.
When her pointy fingers welcome you in,
There's nothing now that can save you from sin.

Bit by bit, envy will tear you apart,
You can't stop now, this is just the start!
Battling against a stormy sea,
It seems the whole world is pitched against me!

When you hear the green worm whisper in your ear,
'Get me that now, don't you hear?'
Jealousy lies out in the dark
And when it's time, it strikes like a great shark.

Envy is as fierce as a tiger
So don't trust it for it's a liar!

Emma McAfee (10)
Bushvalley Primary School, Ballymoney

Fury

He lives where no other emotion will challenge him,
Where the fire, lava and smoke
Will all make you choke;
Fury lives deep inside your fist and feet.

He is the outrage when left out of games,
He is like a bull stumping,
Forcing you to lose your rag;
Fury goes on a rampage when he's hurt.

His friend, Anger, lives in the same
downhearted valley,
Where they often meet in the valley
With the other evil emotions;
Fury is waiting for you in the Valley of Shadows.

Elisha Van Der Byl (10)
Bushvalley Primary School, Ballymoney

Mr Rage

Oh Mr Rage, why must you be so cruel and mean?
You shout and scream but can't be seen.
I know when you are coming,
I can feel it in my tummy -
My fists all crunch
And I want to punch!
I try to hide you deep inside,
But you shriek and moan,
That's followed by a groan.
Wait, I know what'll silence you -
Love and care, that's what I'll do
So you won't be seen for a few more days.
You can't always have your way.
There shall be peace at last
And I can relax and think about what's passed.

Abigail Jane Sayers (10)
Bushvalley Primary School, Ballymoney

Happiness

It's lazing on the beach on a warm summer's day,
It's no one but me and my family together,
It's a warm feeling deep inside,
Everyone should have happiness in their life.

It's a thing that people enjoy,
When he comes out it's the best of all.
He lives in the sun and plays in the grass,
He can save you from your worries and doubts.

He can take care of your illness,
He can battle your weaknesses,
He is kind and fun,
He is Happiness.

Mark Chestnutt (11)
Bushvalley Primary School, Ballymoney

Worry

Worry is one of the most terrible emotions,
Worry comes out of her hiding place
When you move to a new school
Or have forgotten a maths question,
She can also suddenly appear as you swim!

Worry lives in darkness deep down,
Where monsters roam -
How can you call that home?

Worry is as green as a sick sailor
And is as scared as an elephant when it
spots a mouse!
Don't let her get to you and you'll be fine
Please trust me,
I've met her too many times!

Erin Armstrong (10)
Bushvalley Primary School, Ballymoney

Happiness

Happiness comes out when everyone is merry,
She fights off fear because it's scary.
Happiness is like the sun, always ready to play,
I like to be happy at the end of the day.

Happiness lives in your heart
And you never want it to part,
But sometimes anger drives it away
When it wants to come out and play.

Happiness is like a bird flying free,
It is so light-hearted, it fills me with glee.
I would like my happiness to stay
And never have reason to keep at bay.

Adam James Feeney (10)
Bushvalley Primary School, Ballymoney

POETRY EMOTIONS - The Joys Of Life

Joy

This is Joy.
She lives in the fluffiest of clouds
And plays in the happiest of memories.
She loves to holiday and win the cutest of puppies.
Joy hates the sadness of losing a friend
On whom you once thought you could depend.

This is Joy.
Joy is a blue sky on a summer's day
And puppies playing with a favourite toy.
Joy makes you the happiest you have ever been.
Her friend is the delight of a soft, cold ice cream.
Joy is the most delightful emotion of all.

Kurt Wright (11)
Bushvalley Primary School, Ballymoney

Joy

Joy's wishes for you
Are kind hearts, shining souls,
Smiling greatly, happy glee.

Joy is found
Inside your soul
And seeps to the surface
When you need it most.

Joy feels like
Your heart singing
Your feet dancing
Floating on a breeze.

Paula Lamont (11)
Bushvalley Primary School, Ballymoney

Joy

Joy is a dream on a summer's day,
Lying on a lounger,
Smiling all day,
Listening to music,
I'm happy all day.

Joy is when it's time to play,
Singing a song,
It's a chat with a friend,
A kind word,
My favourite feeling.

Jill Stirling (10)
Bushvalley Primary School, Ballymoney

Jealousy

Jealousy is birthed when you are greedy
When it comes you will want
All the things you see.

It will slowly, so slowly, take over your life,
Like a bad dose of flu
On a cold winter's day.

Take care of your emotions
Or you will be absorbed
By the evil force of jealousy.

Brian Patton (10)
Bushvalley Primary School, Ballymoney

Joy

Joy is like lying on the
Beach on a hot summer's day.
Joy lives deep, deep in
Your little heart.
It feels like jumping through
A colourful cloud,
Eating a sweet
And drinking hot chocolate
With marshmallows on top!

Callum Gibson (11)
Bushvalley Primary School, Ballymoney

Pleasure

Pleasure lives in joyful things
And loves to have jollity
But lives an anxious life and she will stay
Far away from eternity.

She loves the day when school's out,
Messing around when summer's about!
She likes to see a cloudless sky
While munching on a custard cream pie.

Alex Christie (11)
Bushvalley Primary School, Ballymoney

Happiness

People lying on a beach under a blue sky,
Sunbathing on the smooth sand,
Smoothing on sun cream as they tan
Under a ball of fire - that's happiness.

Listening to the waves crashing
As they splash on the yellow sand,
The children laughing at the approach
Of the ice cream van - that's happiness.

Ellie McFadden (11)
Bushvalley Primary School, Ballymoney

Jealousy

Jealousy is that feeling deep in your side,
Where no other emotion lives.
It's hard to get rid of once it's there.
Joy is the enemy of Jealousy,
They battle day and night.
Let the joy in, let it win.

Bailey Ayres (10)
Bushvalley Primary School, Ballymoney

Worry

The worry emotion is found deep in your heart.
It can make you feel upset.
If you cry with worry tell someone -
I am sure they will help you not to be down.
Don't worry about things, it will all be fine
In a day or a week we won't see your frown.

Matthew Craig (10)
Bushvalley Primary School, Ballymoney

Gone Forever

I'm so sad,
When I'm bad.
Because I know I've broken the one rule.
All my other friends tease me,
Because I can't catch the ball.
At the weekend I'm free,
I don't have to catch the ball,
Break the one rule,
Or even get teased.
I just be myself, with her.
But they shout and scream,
When I have a dream.
The only person who can help me is her.

Only the car just flew past,
It's all over and too late.
She's gone forever!
Right now I taste stale bread.
Everything I look at turns different shades of blue.
I hear laughing and then her voice telling them to leave me alone.
Tears leaking from my eyes,
I feel like Andy Murray when he's lost a game.
I lost something today, more of a someone; my best friend.
We might be able to communicate,
But she will always be in my heart.
Wherever she is, we are still together.

Georgia Moore (11)
Cedars Park Primary School, Stowmarket

Lifeless

I'm isolated,
Who knows,
Who understands,
What my life,
Is worth.

Beneath my soul,
Is a black hole,
Swallowing my life,
As time goes.

The uproar,
The spruce waves,
Overwhelm my heart,
For it drowns,
Down and down.

Until my eyes have no pupil,
Filled with cloud grey.

The lemonade skin,
Soon looks like a bin,
The colour,
So pewter,
So dull.

My life,
Tastes like,
Water,
Nothing.

The killer galaxy,
Takes over the hole,
In my heart.

The journey of,
Death,
Isn't too painful!

Millie Bayes (11)
Cedars Park Primary School, Stowmarket

Fearful

I'm a light shade of pistachio green
An overwhelmed sky blue
That's all . . .

I will sprinkle across the world
I will run across the world
I will paint the world
I will smother the world
I will . . .

Everyone will shiver
Like a tree
Butterflies will fly
In their stomach
Everyone hates me

I will sprinkle across the world
I will run across the world
I will paint the world
I will smother the world
I will . . .

The world is a one way road
You can never turn back
You can never stop to look around
This is me . . .

I will sprinkle across the world
I will run across the world
I will paint the world
I will smother the world
I will . . .

Families will be broken
Part by part
All because of me . . .

Lily Ruscoe (11)
Cedars Park Primary School, Stowmarket

Pressure

It's a deep ocean blue,
Creating waves,
As heavy as an elephant,
It makes you pray.

It sits atop your shoulders
And keeps adding weight,
Until you crumble beneath it,
And have to give way.

It won't come off,
It grips you tight,
It feels like sandpaper,
Rubbing your mind.

It is like bubblegum,
Sticky and annoying,
You blow your bubble,
And try to hold it,
But it eventually goes pop.

It hits you when you least expect it,
When you're making a decision or choice,
It crushes you,
Your life is a misery.

If you get it,
You won't be able to think.
It creates a black hole,
Where a mind used to be.

It warps you,
And makes you change,
And before you know it,
You're not the same.

Jack Atkins (10)
Cedars Park Primary School, Stowmarket

Disgusted And Delighted

Dark red, dark green,
Black like coal in the deepest hole,
These colours represent . . .
Chalkboard sounds, high-pitch opera,
These are the sounds that make me . . .
Wet socks, wet dogs and mouldy eggs,
These are the smells that go with . . .
As spicy as chili, as disgusting as Turkish Delight
And black liquorice,
These are the tastes of . . .

As blue as the sky on a summer day,
As yellow as a juicy lemon,
As pink as a cute pig,
And as purple as an aubergine.
As fluffy as candyfloss,
As fluffy as a cat,
As fluffy as a pure white clouds.
As sweet as sugar,
As sugary as sweets.
Smells like fresh baked cakes,
Like warm melted chocolate.
Sounds like an ice cream van on a hot day
Or a cat purring happily.
What am I?

Kenzie Springall (11)
Cedars Park Primary School, Stowmarket

Anxiousness

I jump around as happily as ever,
If only this could last forever.
Suddenly I land on the grass,
My world flips around and dark feelings harass.

I sit surrounded by staring eyes,
It seems like my good feelings were just lies.
This feeling tightens all around me,
Is this really how it has to be?
It jumps around me as I turn inside out,
I wish that I could spit it out.

As me and my unwelcomed companion meet,
I feel as if I am chewing on something I don't want to eat.
Can't someone put out a hand and take me away.
Maybe then my nightmares will end
And I will be able to find the light of day.

Faint whispers enter my mind,
like humming and hissing combined.
I wish that I could yell,
Let everyone know about how I fell.
Someone needs to crash this gate,
For this is what keeps me a happy fate.

Paulina Latka (11)
Cedars Park Primary School, Stowmarket

Sadness

Sadness is the colour blue like a balloon, going into the sky.
I felt sad the first time I saw my new dog.
Because my old dog had died.
I still miss him.

Sadness is an emotion never happy,
Always the opposite of joy.
Sadness tastes like dirt!

Toby Isaacs
Cedars Park Primary School, Stowmarket

POETRY EMOTIONS - The Joys Of Life

Tearful Test

All you can hear is *drip, drop, drip, drop,*
On her top.
Letting my emotions run free,
All it comes down to is the final results.
Worried about your test?
Well just do your best!
Panicking does not help,
Just practise and practise and practise.

When it comes to the day,
The colour is grey.
The taste is salty
But believe me it is not as frightening as swimming with sharks.
However, if you give up, you might trip up.
And fail the test completely.
All you can hear is *tick, tock, tick, tock,*
Whatever you do, don't look up at the clock.

I'm warning you whatever you do, don't look at the clock!
Knowing how much time you have,
Does not help you at all.
Don't let your tears free,
What emotion could I be?

Molly Mayhew (10)
Cedars Park Primary School, Stowmarket

Worried

As blue as a blueberry
Like a mysterious thumping noise
Like the sound of my heart beating

It is a sprinting smell of fear
As precious as a diamond lying silently
At the bottom of a caramel coloured canyon.

I hope no one will fear me again.

Savannah Cross (10)
Cedars Park Primary School, Stowmarket

Relieved

A glittering silver, shining as bright as the moon,
The taste of clear water coming soon,
When the war was over, when they found the code,
This feeling kept on the road.
Like the air coming out a balloon after it was full,
This feeling makes you feel tall,
A breath of fresh air,
To every truth and dare,
You will feel this once it's over.

No more bombs,
No more deaths,
No more guns,
And no more war.
It's all over,
Water is in hot countries,
People coming back to their families after the war,
Peace comes between countries,
Your family got through an illness,
Jewish people are safe,
Everyone is filled with the same emotion,
Relief . . .

Jessica Terrell (10)
Cedars Park Primary School, Stowmarket

POETRY EMOTIONS - The Joys Of Life

Football Feelings

My team is Ipswich, they will never be ditched.
When we lose,
You hear all the boos.
Our team is losing quite a lot,
Knocked out of the cup,
Such a big loss.
They're really disappointing me, but there is so much more to see.
The cheers when we score with skill,
Backfired when we lose 3-0.
Persevere, block the fear,
Home or away, winning is near.
Come on Ipswich! Turn the game around,
Or people's anger will be wound.
Losing has not been great,
It seems to me that it's too late.
But I can't lose hope,
I have to cope.

Morgan Cansdale (11)
Cedars Park Primary School, Stowmarket

Emotions

The pen just keeps on tap, tap, tapping,
Against your perfect, pearly teeth.
A man in the black cloak,
Jumps on the tool,
Custard and burnt toast tagging along,
Not wanting to be left behind.
Because the man in the black cloak is the 'cool one',
The one everyone wants to be with . . .
Not against.

Silly questions sprint around the track,
Inked inside your brain.
It's the friends that ask these questions,
Not the mean at heart.
But all of this adds up,
Helping anger on his way,
Up, up, up is where he goes.

What emotion am I?
A: Annoyance.

Emma Balaam (11)
Cedars Park Primary School, Stowmarket

Hopeless

I cannot do anything anymore,
My life is such a bore.
I just taste like a stale cracker,
Bland, dry, tasteless.

I don't smell fresh,
I smell like strong coffee.
I need help, somebody help.
Now, quick, too late.

If you touch me I don't move,
Still, finished, done.

Elizabeth Elmer (10)
Cedars Park Primary School, Stowmarket

POETRY EMOTIONS - The Joys Of Life

Excitement

Your eyes flicker open, you don't know what's happening,
You can't remember what day it is, you can't remember that it's your special day.
Then suddenly you remember,
And you scream, 'Yes!'
You scuttle out of bed, and take a look a the time on your phone.
'4.30,' you say to yourself, 'eh, I can wake them up.'
You skip to your parents' room, giddy with excitement.
'Let's go!' you say.
They rub their eyes and flop down to sleep.
You run downstairs, two steps at a time.
You feel jolly, skippy, jumpy and lucky at the same time,
You cannot
That feeling when you know you're going to get tons of presents
That feeling when you're too excited, you feel like you could burst.
It's the best feeling ever.

Ellie Ames (10)
Cedars Park Primary School, Stowmarket

Frustration

A dark purple colour comes from under the locked door,
Click, click, click - over and over and over again,
A bitter taste meets your taste buds,
A burnt smell whiffs across the room,
There's a storm in your head,
It's raging on,
Your head's about to explode.

Your heart is like a hammer,
Smashing the storm to shards,
Your blood boils like Bangladesh,
Your headache is like an earthquake.

What emotion am I?

Harry Coffey (11)
Cedars Park Primary School, Stowmarket

Confused

An unsure brick red,
rushing through your head,
you don't know what to do,
except you can see mist.

The smell of burning ash,
running up your nose,
a horrible scent,
making you think.

It tastes like lemon and lime,
sweet but sour,
drifting down your mouth,
making you even more unsure.

It sounds like several people thinking,
standing still and never blinking,
always thinking,
but why?

Kody Thomas (11)
Cedars Park Primary School, Stowmarket

POETRY EMOTIONS - The Joys Of Life

Sad Memories

Turquoise, light blue, are the colours I feel,
Bringing in all the smells of reminded meals,
Cheese sauce, gammon and lots more,
Watching the waves at Felixstowe shore.

My tears fall down my face,
I remember going to an amazing place,
Going to Disneyland, having fun,
Playing in the yellow sun.

I remember when I was small,
I remember being cool,
Playing at the park with my dad,
I remember I was never sad.

But now my emotions are just filled with sadness,
No happiness in my life.
Now I'm sad forever,
Being sad because of my life.

Louise Blair (11)
Cedars Park Primary School, Stowmarket

Lonely

Magenta is not the
colour that describes my feelings
pewter grey is the correct one.

I feel as if the world
flashed before my eyes.
My world is crushed.

It's like bread without butter,
fish without chips,
pasta without sauce and
crackers without cheese, bland.

This is the worst feeling,
the world is a one way road
I can never turn back.
The world is no longer my oyster . . .

Rosie Ager (11)
Cedars Park Primary School, Stowmarket

Creeped Out!

It was in the middle of the night,
Something spooked my night,
The door slammed shut!
It gave me a fright.

In my mind I saw the colour dark purple,
I felt like I was in a haunted house,
I felt I was in a dream,
Was I?

It tasted like I'd just eaten a bug!
Maybe it wasn't a dream,
I had this feeling it wasn't.

Can you guess what I am?
My name is Creeped Out!

Kate Marie Chapman (10)
Cedars Park Primary School, Stowmarket

Fear

The last tear hits the floor,
A decision is made,
But why? you ask.

The water floods in,
Explosions rattle the stricken ship, Stukas screaming from left, right and centre
People screaming, crying and praying.

Bodies strewn across the deck,
I made a choice
A hard choice.

Are soldiers more important than civilians?
The ship sinks because of me,
Put yourself in my perspective,
It's either kill or be killed . . .

Kian Patel (10)
Cedars Park Primary School, Stowmarket

Frustration

A burning shade of scarlet red,
This is the only colour in my head.
Raging red faces all in hate,
No one seems to care about their fate.

Feels like fire is coming out of your ears,
The continued sound of thunder is all anyone hears.
How do people live with all this anger?

The smell of smoke,
Tastes of dry oak.
Smoke from the worst bonfire,
Oak from the biggest, roughest tree.

Anyone who feels this emotion,
Don't worry, you're under my potion.

Chloe Leeder (10)
Cedars Park Primary School, Stowmarket

Be Happy When You're Sad

Don't let the sadness get to you, be happy
think of sweet, zesty fruit, the smell of freshly picked flowers
Yellow, think of yellow, the fun, happy colour.
Think of birds chirping, maybe go to the beach.
But don't be sad!
Hearing the waves crashing against the rocks
But don't be sad!
Sunbathe, don't sit in a cave
Buy a ball from the mall
The sky might be grey but think of a new day
So don't be sad!
Read a book or go to New Look
Have a drink from the sink
But don't be sad.
Remember, don't be sad!

Mia Turner (11)
Cedars Park Primary School, Stowmarket

Pressure

I'm an ash taste,
a crimson red,
and a subtle scream.
I'm a motivating hum in your head.

I'm Blu-Tac being stretched,
I am kneaded bread,
I taste like a strong cheese; difficult to bear,
I'm a stone blue.

I'm a copper brown,
A sound of gears grinding together,
I taste like plain water,
And smell like a match being lit.

I'm a force you can't ignore.

Alexander Crawford (10)
Cedars Park Primary School, Stowmarket

Confusion

Am I right?
Am I wrong?
What am I feeling?
Am I feeling a lipstick red?
Maybe.
Am I feeling a sapphire blue?
Possibly.
Am I feeling a fern green?
Probably.
Yes I know now.
I'm feeling confused.
Confusion tastes like the salty sea.
Confusion tastes like blue and green.
It smells like ordinary water.
And sounds like the ocean waves.

Amelia Elizabeth Fokinther (11)
Cedars Park Primary School, Stowmarket

Emotion In Football

Losing a game is hard, but winning . . .
It's just a new beginning.

Dark red anger comes, it spoils your fun
But when you score a goal, it makes you feel special.

When you watch your team win, feelings come in
You want to express so much
But then you lose against the Dutch.

After game, after game, sobbing everywhere
Our team lost hope

I never give up on any football game
I think of my future and fame

What emotion am I?

Luke Beamish (10)
Cedars Park Primary School, Stowmarket

Frustration At Bletchley Park

Frustration filled my mind.
Do I save the 300 soldiers or 100 civilians?
The Germans will bomb their refugees,
Or our soldiers.

Two boats sail the sea
And the German don't know we know.
My mouth tastes like I have just been sick.
A dark red, red as blood, filled my mind.

Tick, tock, tick, tock
Goes the clock,
The Germans have bombed
They killed their own
And my brother.

Hannah May Chevin (11)
Cedars Park Primary School, Stowmarket

Strong

I'm a potent smell of chilli
a graceful taste of apple pie
the colour of lipstick red
a smell of victory for all.

When you push me down
I always rise up
even if I have no luck
The colour of crimson red
makes me powerful.

I am the best
and everyone should know
that I'm the greatest feeling
of them all!

Tara King (11)
Cedars Park Primary School, Stowmarket

Anger!

The burning taste of lava in your mouth,
A candy red lights up my face,
It feels like daggers ripping you apart,
All I can hear is screaming!

Electricity runs through my veins,
A lightning strike,
Teal blue light,
This is what it feels like.

Will this feeling leave me,
Or will it stay for evermore?
My face hurts,
It's scarlet red,
I feel like I just want to explode!

Sophie Norris (11)
Cedars Park Primary School, Stowmarket

Pressurised

Torn between them,
Why two?
Dejected, hopeless and all down to me,
They want it soon.

It is as pitch-black as midnight,
It is a walking burning smell.
It is screaming at me,
It is a silent sizzling yell!

Me and this office chair,
Our lives are very bare.
It could go poor,
Or I could be in awe.

Eloise Jackson (10)
Cedars Park Primary School, Stowmarket

Confused

A rush of bewildering lapis blue,
a swirl of lost azure blue.
A silver sheet of mist,
that mixes everything up.

So many paths,
which one to choose?
A bag of sweet and salty popcorn,
that is always unpredictable.

A strong scent of sweet chili,
leads you different ways.
An endless humming inside your head,
that leads you right back to where you started.

Finley Davis (10)
Cedars Park Primary School, Stowmarket

Relief

The caramel taste hits your mouth,
levels what is coming south,
thinking of the possibilities,
linking all of the certainties.

Success battles all the anger,
trying to leave me with a cliffhanger.
Fighting away the bad demons,
leaving me with good omens.

The buttery shadows leaning over,
speaks to me with a pleasant manner.
Taking me through a world of wonder,
I wonder . . .

Jack Webb (10)
Cedars Park Primary School, Stowmarket

Anger

Anger is an emotion you can't control,
A volcano erupting in my soul,
Climbing, rising from below,
Watch out people I am about to blow!
Here it comes a fiery blast,
Mouth wide open, how long will it last?
Eyes streaming, body shaking,
Even the ground has started shaking.

Ella Thompson (10)
Charlton Primary School, Wantage

Anger

Anger is a fireball swelling in your body,
It will never wait its turn, it will never let you learn,
It is a gun firing in your body,
Anger is a volcano erupting in your mind,
Anger is a boxer taking punches at your mind,
It is a bull charging at your brain,
Anger is a force taking over the world,
Anger is destructive force that needs to be stamped out.

Joseph Quinan (10)
Charlton Primary School, Wantage

Feeling

Fear's the one that gives you worries,
Anger's the one that makes you mad,
Disgust's the one that gives you a style,
Sadness is the one that breaks you apart,
Joy's the one that gives you a heart.
These are all of our different emotions,
That make up who you are.

Olivia Moor (9)
Charlton Primary School, Wantage

Anger

Anger is bold and very big
Your hair goes wild
Your face goes red
Anger is something you can't control
The ground starts shaking
Bang! Boom! Bash!

Jolie Camden (8)
Charlton Primary School, Wantage

Boredom

At school I feel bored
All you hear is groaning and moaning
My mouth looks like a dark abyss
My eyes are closed tightly
My head is floppy and heavy as the world
You barely hear chirping, just murmuring.

Harry Reeves (9)
Divine Saviour RC Primary School, Abbots Langley

What Emotion Am I?

I have a red hot face
As hot as the sun and
My hands are covered with sweat.
Just one drop of it could set
Hundreds of candles alight,
While my throat is as dry as a desert.

What emotion am I?
A: Anger.

Jeffery Guo (8)
Elmlea Junior School, Bristol

Refugee

The swaying of the boat,
Dancing tensely.
The vulnerability of us all,
Agitation pumping.
The promise of relief,
Beaming broadly.

All refugees will stand together,
We will endure forever and ever!
When tyranny is defeated,
We will all be greeted,
With exhilaration,
And life!

The soothing of the mothers,
Selflessness shining.
The compassion for lost ones,
Flowing richly.
The resilience of our people,
Dignity persisting.

All refugees will stand together,
We will endure forever and ever.
When tyranny is defeated,
We will all be greeted,
With exhilaration,
And life!
Exhilaration,
And life!

Evan Baker (10)
Elmlea Junior School, Bristol

Boredom

Boredom lives in travelling,
It's easy to provoke -
Comes out with a heart-dropping moan.

But what do people do when they are bored?
My fingers are twitching,
Body's weary,
The itch on my foot a melancholy burn.

I gaze out at the cars
Shuffling tediously along the road.
I think, *Urgh!*
Is this all life holds?

The weather's gloomy,
Sombre and bleak.
But the grey creates a sullen atmosphere.

The faces of those,
Full of hope,
Ready to be squashed by the traffic.

My mind is like a blank page,
Nothing to distract me from this boredom!
The car's engine is a droning parent.

Finally, we're here!
I can move, I can live again!
My legs are numb, barely alive.

The dull grey monster is at last gone!

Joe Preddy (9)
Elmlea Junior School, Bristol

A Victorian Christmas

It's Christmas Eve and I've still lots to do,
I've got crackers and choir, lots of other things too.
Ma's in the laundry hanging out clothes,
And Pa's in the bathroom washing his toes.
The chimney sweep boy's having his day off,
Right now he's out putting food in the trough.

I've just gone to bed but I'm lying awake,
Tomorrow's the dinner with lots of the cake.
I feel so excited, then I hear a sound,
I sit up and listen, as someone's feet touched the ground.
I think that it's Santa so I dare not go down,
So I just go to sleep, wrapped up in my gown.

The bells are ringing, it's Christmas Day,
I run down the stairs, beaming all the way.
I open my presents, I got a new bonnet,
It's got roses, daisies and buttercups on it.
Pa got a wristwatch, Ma got a shawl,
Sissy got a hoop and Tom got a ball.

Now for dinner my favourite part,
All the family's here, we're having a laugh.
We pulled our crackers with a bang and a pop,
The turkey's got all types of spices on top.
It seems to have gone so quickly, this Christmas Day,
The next is still a very long time away.

Rose O'Brien (8)
Elmlea Junior School, Bristol

Aeroplane Excitement

A t the airport,
I n the queue,
R eally tired of waiting,
P assports passed through,
O nto the escalator,
R unning to
T he departure gate number 23.

A nd onto
E xciting aeroplane,
R eady to go through,
O nto seats 41, 42 and 43
P laying, so excited to fly to
L ovely, relaxing Egypt,
A nd watching the clouds that so beautifully move,
N ot making me less excited though,
E xcitement awaits all those going to

H urghada in Egypt
O ff the plane to
T he coaches
E ager but patient too,
L ook, we've arrived, it's so beautiful!

Eloise Allen (9)
Elmlea Junior School, Bristol

POETRY EMOTIONS - The Joys Of Life

Surprised

Surprised lives in the most unexpected place,
From in your car to in a familiar face,
And sometimes he jumps up without warning,
Which could create fun out of something boring.

Being shocked by something remarkable,
Or something unusual and unpredictable,
It's these things that make Surprised appear.

And when he does his mouth is an elastic band
And has eyes like footballs,
Although he's the sneakiest emotion
You'll probably find him hiding behind the wall,
When he finds you try not to go mad,
Just calm down, you'll never know if it's good or bad.

The only way to recover from the shock
Is to settle down and stare at something peaceful like a rock.
Once he goes you'll realise that it's OK,
You'll probably start doing some ballet,
But before the time you could count to ten,
You will soon be wondering when you'll meet him again.

Ben McIlree
Elmlea Junior School, Bristol

Angry Boy

A nger comes from deep within me,
N iggling and wriggling like a grub in a tree,
G et away, get away, leave me alone,
R eally, it's like a dog with a bone,
Y es, I'm as angry as a volcano about to erupt,

B etter try not to sound awfully abrupt,
O h I must tell myself to take a deep breath,
Y es, and try to focus on starting afresh.

John Suggett
Elmlea Junior School, Bristol

Feline Feelings

They have fur which is black and white,
And eyes that are green and bright,
Cute little noses which are very pink,
And their long tails which trail as they slink.
Away they go, stepping with their paws,
If you are a cat there are no rules.

Jumping as high as a lamp post
And sometimes trying to lick my toast,
They're cheeky little devils they really are,
But they'll never manage to get my whole dinner, hurrah!

So what can those creatures be?
Yes they're cats and they are very silly.
They make me feel many emotions - sometimes that is sad,
Like when I have to go to school, it doesn't make me glad.
But the favourite feeling I feel with my cats
Is amazingly calm and purrfectly relaxed
I know all the cats in the world can't be mine
But they really are so simply divine.

Suki Linstead (8)
Elmlea Junior School, Bristol

My Anger

Small things spark great anger
Blazing, roaring in my ears
Slamming against my head
Screaming to get out
Consuming me in the midst of flames
I feel like fire
Gradually it all dies down, burns up
Peace again.

Mani Cresswell (8)
Elmlea Junior School, Bristol

POETRY EMOTIONS - The Joys Of Life

How Do I Feel?

How do I feel when it's warm and sunny?
I get a tingling in my tummy,
How do I feel when it's windy and cold?
I snuggle down with my daddy bold.

How do I feel in a thunderous din?
It makes me jump out of my skin,
When lightning flashes like Superman dashes,
It makes me scared of everything.

How do I feel when the hail pelts down?
I stare in awe as it whitens the town.
How do I feel when the wind howls a treat?
I'm excited - I might be blown off my feet!

How do I feel when the heavens open?
When the rain pours down I feel broken,
When the rainbow appears in the bright blue sky,
I sing hallelujah and throw my hands up high.

Alex Peter Morris (9)
Elmlea Junior School, Bristol

Lady Calm

Lady Calm comes when you've had a good time,
When you're sweaty and excited,
But it's time to calm down.

She smoothes her silky-soft hands over you,
Soothing the ripples of excitement that rise in your mind.

She weaves the spell of heavy eyelids and sleepiness,
Then casting the net over you
Like a blanket while you lie in bed.

Her sweeping robes are crystal white,
Her chestnut hair as glossy as a horse's flank,
She holds a shining silver star of hope,
Cradling it in her gentle hands.

And although her face may seem still,
If you look carefully, deeply, into her dark, dark eyes,
You will see that they are full of twinkling stars.

Anna Mahon (10)
Elmlea Junior School, Bristol

Hunger

I come out when an earthquake strikes
Me and Anger are mates for days and nights
I am never stuffed
Food never gives me enough
The other emotions are afraid of me
And others don't get enough of me
I can easily say
I could eat a whale
I'm as hungry as a goat
And even more!
I could eat a boat!
So if you see me, beware!
I could eat you before you're there!

Alex Davidson (8)
Elmlea Junior School, Bristol

POETRY EMOTIONS - The Joys Of Life

Insecurity

I suppose it's when you feel helpless, vulnerable, exposed to the world.
A rather nasty feeling really.
People seem scary, threatening even.
You just don't know why but you feel sad, melancholy, nothing.
Everything seems to make you want to cry and cry and cry
Until you feel even emptier than you already do.
Words said are like arrows piercing you, making you angry,
Lashing out like a wounded bear.
You just want to be alone so that you can't hurt anybody.
You long for sleep to calm you
Like a long, welcoming, enveloping hug.
And in the morning all the fog will have lifted
And you feel bright,
Confident,
Truly alive again.

Lucy Ashworth
Elmlea Junior School, Bristol

Tennis Tournament Turmoil

Hiding under the covers, I didn't wish to wake,
Today was my tennis tournament - I wished I could escape.
The rumbling of the car engine disturbed my troubled thoughts
And after what seemed like an eternity we arrived at the tennis courts.

When I looked at the match sheet, I saw I was playing a boy
And in my stomach I felt the opposite of joy.
I longed for some interruption - something to cause delay,
But then I heard the referee say, 'Get ready to play!'

My hands were trembling as we started the game,
What if I lost, I'd feel such shame.
After a struggle, we were finally done,
What a wonderful feeling - I had actually won.

Zoey Yan Starke (10)
Elmlea Junior School, Bristol

Happiness

Happiness lives everywhere,
Where flowers and rainbows are,
She always comes out with joy
And loves to go 'ha ha'.

Being fun in games or making new friends,
Or eating ice creams,
These are the things that make Happiness appear
And she'll laugh and be on everyone's team.

She is joyful to see,
She's the kindest emotion around,
Everyone loves her - they all come to play,
As she's the nicest sound.

So try to keep Happiness by smiling each day
And Happiness will pay you with kindness.

Emily Inch
Elmlea Junior School, Bristol

Hunger

I'm as hungry as a hyper hippo,
And for tea I want
Pizza with scrummy toppings,
Ice cream as cold as snow,
Cake with a rich creamy chocolate centre,
Chips stained red with ketchup,
And seas of hot chocolate that is real brown lava.

Ten long minutes later,
Happiness floods through me,
I hear a call saying, 'Dinner time!'
Don't bother washing my hands,
I hear the clash of the pots and pans,
But what's on my plate?
Cold cabbage stew!

Lucy Regan (10)
Elmlea Junior School, Bristol

POETRY EMOTIONS - The Joys Of Life

Angry As A Bull

Anger is like a steaming bull
Charging at a red flag
Or a roaring, raging river
Ripping against the banks
Anger is like a stormy sky
Lighting up the night
Or a giant dragon
Furious, fiery, fierce.

Being teased
Foul tackling
Broken promises
These things make me angry
Deep breaths, count to ten
Anger slowly disappears.

Sebastian (8)
Elmlea Junior School, Bristol

I Am Anger

I live in the darkest places.
My skin is burning hot.
I blow up everything in my sight,
But I care not.

My teeth are razor-sharp fangs,
Hunting for their prey.
I have fire glowing in my eyes
And eyebrows black as coal.
Perfect claws I have,
For digging deep dark holes
And trapping people.
Then my feeling enfolds.

I am Anger.

Sam Bristow (8)
Elmlea Junior School, Bristol

The Meaning Of Joy

Joy lives in Heaven,
Where sunshine and sweets play,
And sometimes she comes outside unexpectedly,
For a laugh and a trampolining day.

Being told that you're funny,
Or seeing the Easter bunny,
Are things that will make Joy come out.
When she does, she'll laugh with excitement
And giggle with glee.

Her face is bright yellow and her skin is smooth,
And she's the nicest emotion around.
Everybody likes her, they all come and hug her
And will go away when she goes back home.

Lottie Lewis (10)
Elmlea Junior School, Bristol

I Feel Isolated

I feel isolated . . .

Like I am a picture in a frame,
Locked away from humans and contact with anything in the world.
Like I will just lock myself away forever
And not see daylight again.

I feel anger . . .

My blood starts to boil,
I just want to let it out,
I feel like I just want to rip out my hair
But now I know how the teacher feels.

I feel proud . . .

I feel like I can do anything,
I feel like I am on top of the world and I can fly.

Ellis Robson (11)
Gatten And Lake Primary School, Shanklin

Summer Emotions

The day dawned and I woke up
It was the first day of my six week summer!
The excitement fizzed inside
And my whole body felt light.

I went to the play park and saw my friends
As the sun glowed and the sky bent
I went on the slide and the swings
I really felt so happy.

When I came home my bike was gone
And suddenly sadness dawned
Mum hated to see me so blue
But I loved my bike, she didn't have a clue.

When I cheered up, we went to the beach
I had an ice cream and a sweet
When I saw a little boy on my bike
I was burning angry!

I asked for it back, nicely at first
But his dad looked cross and said a bad word
I was scared, what would happen now?
When a nearby policeman turned around . . .

He got me my bike back, and I felt proud
My feet could have been floating off the ground
I rode my bike all the way home
I was ready for a bath, full of foam.

I was tired when I snuggled in bed
Tomorrow I'll relax instead
What an adventure today had been!
I'd had some fun and caught a thief!

Molly Faithfull
Gatten And Lake Primary School, Shanklin

How Sadness And Love Came Together

Valentine's Day full of love and happiness
But a sad day for me
And my family.
One night
I can still remember the fright.
My mum sat me down,
All I could think about was a clown
In my head
Haunting me in bed.
A tear ran down her face
That's all that I could trace
About what she was going to say that day.
She just came out and said it
That my nan had died.
So I went upstairs and cried.
I loved her very much and I still do.
I wish I could have seen her one more time
Cos now I'm feeling blue.
Now she's in the sky.
Heaven's the best place
Where she can live peacefully there.
Looking over us
So we don't come to harm
She was the kindest nan alive.
Nan, I love you
And I know you love me too.

Molly Bennett
Gatten And Lake Primary School, Shanklin

POETRY EMOTIONS - The Joys Of Life

The Brave And Proud Feelings

People feel brave when they have done
Something that they didn't think they could do
People feel proud when they have done
Something really well and found it fun.

I felt brave when I went hacking on my horse
On the road without being on a lead rein
My horse was as good as gold
But my mum's horse is a little bit old.

I felt proud when I had a riding lesson
On my other horse
And did quite well of course!

Everyone can be brave but they can also be proud
Most people feel different things
Without being in a big crowd.

Some people may feel small
But others may feel nothing at all
Some may also feel sad
Because some people have been bad.

Caitlin Dologhan (9)
Gatten And Lake Primary School, Shanklin

Annoying Brother

I have a little annoying brother who is
called Baby Blue,
He hates other little brothers, especially from
little skinny mothers,
He likes to be very naughty and he never goes away,
Today he had a special day and he never went away,
I think that he should get grounded,
He thinks he's hounded,
So let him sleep,
In so deep.

Madison Lexi Collins (8)
Gatten And Lake Primary School, Shanklin

Love Will Never Be

In the classroom, all alone
Soon a prince will show.
Through the door, here he comes,
My true love.
When he first walked in I could not bear
To look and stare.
His hair flipped and a smile
On his face glared.
His lush, luminescent eyes looking at me.
Soon it will be me.
Everywhere I go he's there.
He calls me names but I don't care,
If he's mean I still love him,
It is meant to be.
Then he said to leave him alone
And I cried and cried
And went home.
I know my dream is crushed,
I've had enough!

Maddison Kim Elizabeth Harrop (10)
Gatten And Lake Primary School, Shanklin

A Great Party

M y big day
Y ou're all kind

B est friends forever
I 'm so happy
R iding horses
T hank you
H appy day
D ay for fun
A ll of your friends
Y our funny friends.

Lauren Brooke Riordan Moore (10)
Gatten And Lake Primary School, Shanklin

POETRY EMOTIONS - The Joys Of Life

The Bad Boys

One day I was sad,
I was lonely and slightly mad,
My friends were playing cars,
While I was playing with jam jars.

I said, 'Can I play?
But they said, 'Just go away.'
The next day I went to school
And in the playground they were slightly cruel.

I went back home to see my mum,
I told her about them
But she just said, 'Fill your tum and you'll be done.'

The next day I went to school,
I took my teddy, I called him Tool,
They smashed it, they pulled and kicked too,
Then I said, 'Get away from Tool.'

They ran and ran away from Tool,
And then we went to swim in a pool.

Charlie Cule (8)
Gatten And Lake Primary School, Shanklin

Scared Every Day

Everyone is mean, I wish they could go,
They all make me feel low.
I wish I could give them a punch,
Or maybe throw my lunch!

One day at school,
All of them were cruel.
The main person who is a bully is Billy,
In the class he is very, very silly.

I always get scared when they're near me,
I just want them to disappear!

Tegan Leigh Brown (9)
Gatten And Lake Primary School, Shanklin

The Football Match

One day I had a football match to play.
We had to train before the match.
We started and the other team chanted come on.
Now our team was coming close to the goal.

And I was so excited to be invited to be passed to,
Then I shot and I scored.
I was so proud, the crowd were loud.

Then I scored another and another
Then I saw my mother.
After all my other players scored
The final score was poor for the other team.
It ended out at 9-0 to us
And my friend was being funny
Like a bunny.

Then we had a man of the month
And it went to me.
And that was a very happy day!

Fraser Lloyd (8)
Gatten And Lake Primary School, Shanklin

My Auntie Had Cancer

Sitting beside that hospital bed
All I feel is much dread.
She says, 'I love you,' and holds my hand
Now all I feel is really bland.
I see her eyes close and then I know.
She has died.
Tears run down my face and everyone cries,
Please Auntie, look down on me.
I will always remember you
So always remember me.

Lewis Brand
Gatten And Lake Primary School, Shanklin

My Exciting Birthday

My birthday, what a brilliant day,
I love to celebrate in every way,
I feel so excited when everyone arrives,
It makes me feel surprised.

Stay up all night,
Until it is light,
The sun is very bright,
It's been an exciting night.

I love playing party games,
If they're not lame,
I love jelly and ice cream,
What a dream.

The time I hate the most,
Is when everyone has to go home,
I know I've had a fun time,
I can't wait for my birthday to come again.

Jessica Jayne Cooper (9)
Gatten And Lake Primary School, Shanklin

The Happier You Are

When I'm happy I'm always clappy
And laugh so much it tickles!

My mum and dad are so glad,
When I learnt to ride my bike.

I'm happy when I'm at my dad's at the weekend.
I wish the fun would never end.

We go for walks along the beach
And when we're there we get an ice cream each.

I'm happy when I go to the shop with my pocket money,
I spend it on sweets and they taste yummy.

Bobby Curtis (9)
Gatten And Lake Primary School, Shanklin

A Dream

I woke up in the morning, another boring morning,
A morning like no other but still a boring morning,
Until I opened the curtains, I was bored out of my mind,
The curtains slid open and I saw the bright blue sky.
I shouted to my neighbour but there was no reply
So I looked out of the window, I saw the flying birds
And I wanted to be like them, flying
At that very moment I began to fly
I had a wave of happiness
Even though I didn't know what was going on.
I began to sing a song, a song of happiness
And as I began to drop I began to wake
And when I closed my eyes I was there,
In my room and a world so boring.
I was so angry and sad
That there was no world like that
So another day came.

Leon Philips King (11)
Gatten And Lake Primary School, Shanklin

Christmas

C hristmas is the best time ever
H aving fun makes me feel happy
R iding my scooter makes me smile
I love my Christmas dinner, it makes my tummy happy,
  I have a lot of stuff.
S tocking was full of chocolates
T ime whizzes by on Christmas Day
M y dog and I went for a walk, it made me hungry
A nd I rode on my scooter
S ome of my presents were brilliant.

Caitlin Birtwistle (8)
Gatten And Lake Primary School, Shanklin

POETRY EMOTIONS - The Joys Of Life

Anger

Very deep underground,
Where bad feelings can be found,
Anger lives desperately,
Trying to break free,
Pursuing people is its goal,
Sending our brains out of control,
Anger is a tornado inside,
A feeling that you can't hide,
It's a tornado brewing inside me,
A feeling you want to let free,
Anger makes you want to scream,
Anger, a feeling, is oh so mean,
A light is lit, burning inside,
A feeling that you can't hide,
But anger can be fixed easily
Because calming down is the key.

Amber-Rae Adkins-Hughes (10)
Gatten And Lake Primary School, Shanklin

Summer

S mile at the sunny sun, it makes me feel happy
U nder the parasol trying to keep cool
M aking daisy chains
M agnificent newborn chicks
E ager children queuing up for ice cream.
R ed bulbs opening up,

S izzling sun burning everything in sight,
U se a fan to keep cool at night,
N ew lambs are born.

Benjamin Mark Moralee (8)
Gatten And Lake Primary School, Shanklin

A Bright Day

When it was a bright day
I could see children playing outside
And birds flying in the blue, blue sky.
People, adults running around
To find a shady place to cool down.
I could sit on the window sill
Watching out all day round.
When it was a bright day
I was as happy
As if I had a new family member joining in the fun!
Then I saw a child falling over.
To not ruin the fun I helped her out.
When the bright day drew to a close
The park was empty for sure.
I felt as happy as ever.
Keep smiling!

Kubra Nur Korkmaz (10)
Gatten And Lake Primary School, Shanklin

Anger

Anger is the angry bull inside
Tossing and turning, trying to escape
Anger is an emotion that you can't hold back
And will not make you cake.

Anger is furious, cruel and mean
And will make you wear orange jeans
Anger will make you do bad things
It takes control of you like a puppet
At least that's how it seems.

George Hayward (11)
Gatten And Lake Primary School, Shanklin

Perfect Pooch

I walk into the home,
Hearing barks wherever I roam.
Meeting the breeder opening the door,
A sea of dogs coming more and more.
My parents sat down and I went to play,
Seeing the toys where one dog lay.
The excitement I felt,
I had found my perfect pooch.
I knew he would fit in with Pippa and Looch!
One eye opened,
Greeted by smiling faces.
I knew that we would travel many places.
We took him home and fine he was.
We love him so,
And he looks like Toto from the Wizard of Oz!

Ruby Bodenham
Gatten And Lake Primary School, Shanklin

Happiness On Minecraft

M inecraft is what makes me happy
I am happy defeating the wither
N aughty creepers blow up everything
E very mob will kill Herobrian
C razy craft is awesome
R unaway players never get defeated
A nts should be added
F oals could be awesome
T ea should be added!

Aaron Cooper
Gatten And Lake Primary School, Shanklin

Happy

H appy, it made me snappy,
A nd it was my birthday,
P eople came to my party,
P lease join unicorns clowning around,
I clicked my bells and laughed, 'Ha, ha, ha!'
N ever stopped laughing,
E veryone had a dance,
S illy monkeys jumping over rainbows,
S our Patch Kids are sour.

Abigail Marie Bird
Gatten And Lake Primary School, Shanklin

Silliness

Every day when I'm near a friend I go silly
And when Silliness comes out I go all chilly.
The only way to put Silliness away
Is to put it in the bin.

Sometimes he is weird,
Sometimes he is crazy,
But he is mostly amazing,
But he's mostly very crazy!

Charlie Crabb
Gatten And Lake Primary School, Shanklin

POETRY EMOTIONS - The Joys Of Life

Sad Death

S ad time to be in.
A s I entered the room I was in a sea of tears,
D addy was crying like a baby.

D ying is a sad thing.
E verywhere I had missing pieces.
A place far away,
T hree terrible years have passed,
H appiness is nowhere to be seen.

Alicia Davison
Gatten And Lake Primary School, Shanklin

Happy

I am so happy
I am quite snappy
For the best day ever!
I had to get dressed as quick as a lion
So I could go to Scotland
I had to get up at 5 o'clock in the morning
My mum was shouting as loud as a banging drum
I was dreaming about dripping ice cream.

Ellie Mai Potts (10)
Gatten And Lake Primary School, Shanklin

Rest In Peace

My heart is filled with darkness
I am feeling heartless
My great grandma has died.
The tears dropped down my eyes
I wish these things didn't happen
But unfortunately they just happen.
My sweet, caring grandma,
I hope you rest in peace.

Aiden Dumbleton (10)
Gatten And Lake Primary School, Shanklin

My Guinea Pigs

I have two guinea pigs named Kane and Scruffy.
The day I got them I was overjoyed!
I could have jumped over the moon
Because of how happy I was
But instead . . .
I got them out and played with them instead.
They're the cutest things I know.
The guinea pigs I have at home.

Harry William Byron (10)
Gatten And Lake Primary School, Shanklin

Xmas Has Come!

E ach day you think,
X mas is near,
C oming very close now,
I n the snow you have fun,
T he excitement fills you up,
E very day you will wait until
D *ing-dong* goes the bell and the day has finally come.

Lauren Acons
Gatten And Lake Primary School, Shanklin

The Day Of Sadness

The day I found out
My heart was filled with sadness
My great grandpa had died
I kept all the emotions inside
Because otherwise I would have cried
I have to fly far away
In more than a couple of days
To see him.

Jess Beckley (10)
Gatten And Lake Primary School, Shanklin

Memory Of My Auntie

M y auntie died after we won a football match for the cup
E very year I think of my dad and how he feels about his sister dear
M e, I feel like I'm the only one who can't get over this
O ur favourite time is when we cuddled up on a sofa
R eally I think of cancer like a bug that I don't want!
Y ou know my dad, he is a strong person but he's the best
to get through this.

James Ashley
Gatten And Lake Primary School, Shanklin

Untitled

The angel comes down from the sky
Wraps my heart and I slowly cry
The tears of joy bring happiness to my heart
She took my arms and she just said,
'Come with me up to the sky
Just believe you can fly.'

Doman Madaras
Gatten And Lake Primary School, Shanklin

Winter

W ater is all turning to ice and makes me happy,
I n the snow it's very puffy to make me very jumpy,
N uts being collected by squirrels makes me very fascinated,
T oo cold for ice cream,
E ventually over sadly,
R eady to happen again, hooray!

Kaymen Lee Freddie Cooch (8)
Gatten And Lake Primary School, Shanklin

Spring

S mile at the butterflies flying around me
P erfect day
R oses are so beautiful
I ce cream truck
N ice day for a picnic
G ive a fishing sack to my dad.

Harvey P
Gatten And Lake Primary School, Shanklin

Winter

W ind is beautiful
I ce is very sparkly
N orth Pole makes me cold
T he grass is cold
E xtreme snowball weather
R ecently it was snowing.

Leio Alexander Mellanby-Smith (6)
Gatten And Lake Primary School, Shanklin

POETRY EMOTIONS - The Joys Of Life

In Memory Of My Grandad

M y grandad died when I was only five,
E very year there is a time I cry.
M y nan says he died of old age but I know it was cancer.
O ur favourite game was duck duck goose.
R ena is my nan, she's never upset.
Y es, I'm sad but I remember all of our memories.

Sophie Frewing (10)
Gatten And Lake Primary School, Shanklin

Winter

W hite snow on the ground
I cicles falling
N ice snowmen being made
T ea time is when I have hot chocolate
E ggnog being eaten
R umbling bellies.

Mason Damien Jupe
Gatten And Lake Primary School, Shanklin

Happy Poem For My Dog

When I'm happy it's a nice time.
As long as I don't turn snappy it's usually fine.
I'm getting a dog so I can call it mine,
I think I'm the perfect age, I'm only nine.
I am so happy, I am going to explode,
I am filled with happiness and I mean a load.

Amari Tafari Ralston Blake (10)
Gatten And Lake Primary School, Shanklin

Winter

W inter makes me want to get warm
 I like winter because it snows
N ice people and friends playing in the snow
T ea is always warmer than I like in winter
E gg when it is scrambled I do not like
R unning makes me warm in winter.

Harrison Abbott (7)
Gatten And Lake Primary School, Shanklin

Spring

S pring is my favourite season, it makes me happy,
P eople have fun picnics,
R abbits are cute and fluffy and make me feel all fuzzy,
 I n spring animals are cute and make me feel I want one,
N ew animals are born and make me feel I'm at a farm,
G reen sparkly grass grows and I feel like I'm in bed.

Ava Guy
Gatten And Lake Primary School, Shanklin

Easter

E aster egg chocolate is yummy
A lways eat chocolate eggs
S pecial time
T he Easter bunny delivers the eggs
E verybody eating eggs, that makes me happy
R abbits fluffy and white make me happy.

Logan Shields
Gatten And Lake Primary School, Shanklin

POETRY EMOTIONS - The Joys Of Life

Spring

S pring makes me happy
P laying with my sister, Mia
R abbits, they like carrots
I really like singing
N ot afraid but excited
G reat time playing outside.

Ruby-May Bristow
Gatten And Lake Primary School, Shanklin

What Makes Me Happy

H appy when I'm at my dad's.
A t the park kicking a football.
P laying with my friends on the PS3.
P irate ship at Blackgang Chine makes me happy.
Y ellow reminds me of my birthday.

Lennix James Mellanby-Smith (9)
Gatten And Lake Primary School, Shanklin

The Poem Of Silliness

S illiness can make you happy
I love to be silly and funny
L ove to make people laugh
L ove to play and be mad
Y oung as seven you can be crazy and be yourself.

Ruby Ridgway-Bamford
Gatten And Lake Primary School, Shanklin

Spring

In spring I feel happy.
In spring I feel happy and joyful.
In spring I feel happy, joyful and excited.
In spring I feel happy, joyful, excited and lovely.
In spring my heart feels like it is going to burst with joy.

Evie Thomas
Gatten And Lake Primary School, Shanklin

Love

Love is a friend.
It's not just a friend, it's your life.
It's not just your life, it's your heart.
It's not just your heart,
It's your one in a million.

Ellie Russel (11)
Gatten And Lake Primary School, Shanklin

POETRY EMOTIONS - The Joys Of Life

Tired Cinquain

Tired
When I'm tired
After I run around
I have a drink, I have a sleep
Sleepy.

Toby Page (8)
Gatten And Lake Primary School, Shanklin

Happy

H elpful is being kind and helpful and generous.
A nswers are not silly and not stupid.
P eople are usually and always happy.
P upils are always polite and generous.
Y es people always love to be happy.

Harrison James Chapman (10)
Gatten And Lake Primary School, Shanklin

Amazing World

Disneyland is a magical place,
Where there is only fun.
Once you see it, you will say,
'Mummy, Mummy, I'm not done!'

We saw a nice restaurant,
With characters as soft as a bear.
There was so much more excitement,
I couldn't even bear.
Don't say no to Disneyland,
Don't even dare!

Ridhi Singhagra (7)
International School Of Gabon, Libreville

The Beach

I was at the beach
splashing in the waves.
The wild waves were crushing
to the sand.
I was so scared
that I would drown.
It was loud as thunder.
It was smashing to the shore.
It hit me hard; I was tumbling
and got scratched even more.

Alastair Issei Ruark (7)
International School Of Gabon, Libreville

POETRY EMOTIONS - The Joys Of Life

Ghostly Figure

I was in my house
playing with my Lego,
until it went under the cupboard
and a ghostly figure appeared!
I was sooooo frightened;
It was as white as wind.
I asked my brother to get my Lego
But when he found it,
He didn't see the black shadow.

Jeremy Kei Ruark (7)
International School Of Gabon, Libreville

My Bed

I like my bed, I like it! It's quite comfortable for me.
You need to try it, you will like it!
I say you will like it!
Try it, I say, you will have sweet dreams!

You can get it in any sweet colours,
It makes no noise,
I'm quite sleepy… I can't wait to get into bed!
I'm so happy, don't make me angry!

Hannah Bruce (8)
International School Of Gabon, Libreville

Nature As A Blessing

Here it comes, the summer breeze,
Over the mountains,
And shivering trees.

Down through the river,
The bird's wings,
Fly as quick as lightning,
As the blessing sings.

The bees buzzing,
And the trees fussing,
The bird hibernating,
The bears finding their prey,
As the nature train travel away.

The trees like sky scrapers,
Crouching over me,
As my head looks up high,
Right into the sky,
I see the clouds,
As fluffy as cotton wool,
Giving me a sense of hope,
A sense of joy,
a sense of nature!

Mishal Baig (8)
Iqra Slough Islamic Primary School, Slough

POETRY EMOTIONS - The Joys Of Life

Life As A Blessing

The old man heard the beep
He wished he could once again leap
He wanted to have one more go
He wondered when he could feel the snow
Why couldn't he have one more day, to stay and play
He wanted to ask above because
He knew about God's constant love
He wanted to be young
He wanted to come out
He wished he could have sprung
All the colourful memories running back
How he wished he was young
When his children were roses grown in concrete gardens
He could play like a kid
It was easy for him to open a lid
And now look at him . . . all old and frail
He couldn't even answer the mail
When the blessing was on his bones he could easily eat cones!

How he had hope for his children to have long, fun days
The old man heard the beep . . . *Beep! Beep! Beep!*
And that was the last of that sound.

Nusayba Yusuf (8)
Iqra Slough Islamic Primary School, Slough

85

I Asked The Canal

'Why do you sing,' I asked the canal, 'such an innocent and merry tune?'
'Because,' the canal said, 'I'm having dinner with the lake at noon!'

'Why do you smile?' I asked the canal.
'Because I like relaxing for a while.'
Then the canal stopped smiling,
His voice was fading and it whispered frustratedly,
'Not again!' as it jumped forward past the green plain
'Why do you sit still and who are you waiting for?'
'There's stuff everywhere and it's blocking my door.'
'What is this stuff which is blocking your door.'
'This litter which you kicked to the floor.'

M Fosi (9)
Iqra Slough Islamic Primary School, Slough

Happiness

Happiness is when you are on holiday having fun,
Happiness is when you have a smile on your face, taking a break from school.
Happiness is a smell of delicious, delightful treats,
Happiness is like playing in the garden, shooting goals,
Happiness is like a cupboard, keeping it unlocked is the key;
A taste of happiness is what I imagine Heaven to be!
Happiness is only real if it is shared by giving a smile and showing that you care.
Happiness is happy for everyone!

Anika Jethwani
Jumeirah English Speaking School, Dubai

POETRY EMOTIONS - The Joys Of Life

Henry Bickers . . .

Feels like jumping around like a free lamb, he thinks his dreams
have come true,
He is a bright blooming flower, with a favourite new colour - blue!

It's Henry's first day at his new school, he has many
reasons to be jolly,
He plans to make lots of new buddies, there is so
much happening, holy moly.

There's something else that's very thrilling, he is having
a new baby brother,
He couldn't handle all these things, happening one after another.

He would bounce off walls, as if he has
ants in his pants,
He would chitter chatter all day, keeping everyone
busy with his rants.

Henry was an eager beaver, always in
a colourful mood,
Like a fruit loop in a bowl full of Cheerios, his friends
thought he was a great dude.

Fired-up Henry was ever ready to explode, like the
confetti in a party popper,
Like the water collecting in a sprinkler, hearty Henry
was a real show stopper.

His emotion was like a forest fire, spreading
wherever he went,
The classroom was now buzzing, even when
Henry was absent.

He had gone to the hospital, waiting for his sibling,
Drumming his hands, kicking his legs, pacing
his feet, hopefully wishing.

Finally the baby arrives - his spirits start singing,
Junior Henry Bickers is here, oh the joys
of a new beginning!

Aryav J. Odhrani (8)
Jumeirah English Speaking School, Dubai

Anger, The Fury In Our Body

A ball of fiery light in the darkness,
Like a ball of evil energy in the dark night sky,
Like a never-ending blaze,
Anger, the fury in our body

A trapdoor to another dimension of flames,
An inferno in a heart,
Like a volcano erupting,
Anger, the fury in our body

Like the fury in a storm,
A deadly and dangerous hurricane,
Lava sliding down the side of a volcano,
Anger, the fury in our body

Steam escaping out of a vent,
A bomb exploding,
A wave of hatred,
Anger, the fury in our body

A ghost that spreads hatred,
The scream that cuts through the silence,
The eternal fire in a dragon,
Anger, fury in our body

A river of outrage,
Flames flowing over thunder,
Like an angel of destruction,
Anger, the fury in our body.

Dasuni Gunasekara (8)
Jumeirah English Speaking School, Dubai

Sadness

Grey is the colour that makes me sad
That gives me a feeling of sorrow and dread
When I feel sad my mum feels bad, not at all glad
When I am sad I snuggle up with ted in my bed
Sometimes I get cranky and even a little weepy
My tears roll down and my eyes get seepy
Sadness tastes like a yucky curry
When I am sad my grandma says, 'Cheer up,
don't worry'
When you're sad your heart beats like a drum
And what does my dad do? He drinks rum
Sadness feels like a stormy thunder cloud
Crashing and banging, it's very loud
Then I sit in a corner and start to cry
I think, *Oh happiness bye-bye*
Sadness smells like black burnt toast
And I am sad because my friend just boasts
When I am sad my heart beats fast
I want to eat sweets but my mum will get mad cause it's the last
When I am happy I like to sing
But when I am sad I barely do anything
Sadness looks like a deep dark tunnel
It's more fun to be happier than duller
Sadness, sadness, so, so sad, wish you could
just soar away.

Kiara Dhamecha (8)
Jumeirah English Speaking School, Dubai

Frustration

Frustration is a dark feeling,
It makes you feel defocused . . . anxious . . . horrible,
It camouflages your mind with rage like
an erupting volcano,
You can't stand it! You can't stand it! You can't stand it!

Frustration makes you resentful and hateful,
Unpleasant thoughts and unpleasant feelings,
Frustration is a raging storm inside your head, your heart and your mind,
You can't stand it! You can't stand it! You can't stand it!

Frustration is like a wilted rose,
Its thorns keep pricking on and on,
It hurts . . . it pains . . . it bleeds,
You can't stand it! You can't stand it! You can't stand it!

Frustration takes away your conscience!
Frustration takes away your contentment!
Frustration takes away your confidence!
Frustration takes away your competence!

You're derailed . . . You're depressed . . .
You're demented . . .
You can't stand it! You can't stand it! You can't stand it!

Kiana Sathyanarayanan (8)
Jumeirah English Speaking School, Dubai

Happiness

Happiness is a shining star
Which makes one fly high

You work hard if you are happy
But people think you might be clown-crazy

Happiness is how you feel
Any problem, it helps you deal

If you are happy, you smile
Which takes you miles and miles

Happiness is like a sparkling rainbow
You share it and make other people's faces glow in the form of a bow

Happiness smells like a fresh huge wave
We enjoy and appreciate what we have

It echoes the sound of wind chimes
And life feels like a poem that rhymes

The taste of happiness is like having a bite of a bright colourful rainbow
A time when you jump with joy and let go.

Ishana Khiara (8)
Jumeirah English Speaking School, Dubai

Happiness

Happiness feels like a silk-soft rose
Happiness looks like love
I hear the waves crashing on the sandy beach when I am happy
Happiness feels like fresh doughnuts from the oven
Happiness tastes like fresh chocolate chip cookies
Happiness is when my cat comes and snuggles up to me in bed
Happiness is when my sister gives me
hugs and cuddles
Happiness is when I am eating chocolate and devouring the sweet taste
When I'm happy with my family, happiness surges through me
Happiness is when I see my sister in person or on Facetime
When it's my birthday I fizz with excitement for it
At school I can't help but smile
Happiness surges through me when I'm baking
I want to be happy because if we were all sad, life would be miserable
If people were not happy we would hate our birthdays
Happiness is one of the most powerful emotions, it can defer any other emotion
Just stay calm and smile.

Rebecca Bainbridge (7)
Jumeirah English Speaking School, Dubai

Happiness

Happiness is the colours of the rainbow shimmering across the bright blue sky,
Sometimes laughter reminds you of good memories;
When you are happy you feel glad and free.
Happiness is finding something you have lost,
Happiness is when you get excited
seeing your team win,
Everyone who finds happiness is lucky.

Rania Jethwani (8)
Jumeirah English Speaking School, Dubai

I'll Never Forget

You will always be my friend,
I'll never forget,
Though death did us part.
We'd play footy, games and more,
In his house, my house or the park,
You will always be my friend,
I'll never forget.
It was fast, shocking, scary,
When you were away,
We waited for news day after day,
And heard it at last,
'He's gone.'
Grief, sorrow, sympathy,
Piling on my heart,
But nonetheless, 'He is in a better place.'
I pray, I love, I feel for you,
You will always be my friend,
I'll never forget.
The day has come, his funeral,
Tonnes have gathered.
Piles of red, white and yellow flowers,
By all who loved.
Speeches, stories and our thoughts,
Came crashing on my heart.
The coffin, his body,
Too much sadness for me.
Even though death did us part,
You will always be my friend,
I'll never forget.

Adam Kovalev Brown (11)
Katesgrove Primary School, Reading

My Beloved Friend

Arhant's cute and cuddly
Who's good at footy
And plays with us
Performing successful skills
And rainbow flicks.
He's smart and clever
And will be with us forever
In our hearts and minds
and thoughts and breaths.
In maths he's acute
And has 99 shoots,
He supports Liverpool
and always comes to school
Never late, ever early
he's the best friend I had
till death did us apart.
He had a big smile
and didn't go to the River Nile
he liked the colour green
and was really serene.
He could be cheeky at times,
and sometimes did mime,
He was a story writer
Who wanted to be mightier
in knowledge and in courage,
he never wished to live old age.
His age was eleven,
May he go to Heaven.

Akshay Tumunuri (11)
Katesgrove Primary School, Reading

POETRY EMOTIONS - The Joys Of Life

When You Have To Say Goodbye

When someone you love dearly,
Has to say goodbye,
You get this nervous feeling,
That you just can't hide inside.
For everyone it's different,
Surely, for everyone it's sad?
But for me it's very difficult,
I hope you understand . . .

I'm very, very emotional,
My eyes start to fill up,
I feel something roll down my cheek,
And then I start to frown.
I wish that I never got that feeling,
I start to feel so down,
When someone I loved dearly,
Had to say goodbye . . .
I got the nervous feeling,
And I just couldn't hold it inside.

All those special memories,
Bring smiles upon my face,
I feel happier knowing now,
That you're in a better place.

When I get that nervous feeling,
I try to steer it away,
By remembering all the giggles,
That used to come our way.

Laiba Shafiq (10)
Katesgrove Primary School, Reading

Goodbye

How could I say goodbye to you,
When I had flu,
The pain inside me really hurts,
Can't I go and make desserts?
Everyone was torn apart,
Even inside in the heart.
One day you were here,
The next you disappeared,
What could I have done?
I should have asked everyone!
Maybe I should have ran away,
Or maybe I should have gone to Broadway,
What was I supposed to do?
Go and let the tea brew?

The day we found out wasn't good,
Was the situation misunderstood?
I talked to you in my sleep,
In the morning I would weep,

Days have passed since the death,
Everyone took a deep breath,
If only you came alive,
I would give you a high-five!

How could we say goodbye to you,
When I had flu . . .

Ayusha Shakya (11)
Katesgrove Primary School, Reading

POETRY EMOTIONS - The Joys Of Life

In Memory Of Arhant!

I feel guilty,
It's all my fault,
I couldn't do anything,
It's just tragic,

Why did it happen?
It's as sad as can be,
I feel nothing,
Shame on me,

It all started happening,
Without a warning,
The world stopped . . .
Now to say my goodbye,
Goodbye,
Rest in peace,

You will be here with us,
You will be missed,
Now this is the end,
The end as can be,

He's in a better place,
RIP.

Maizie Rae Townsend (11)
Katesgrove Primary School, Reading

Burning Love

Death leaves a heartache
No one can heal
Love leaves a memory
No one can steal
Those we love
Don't go away
They walk beside us
Every day
Unseen
Unheard
But always near
Still loved
Still missed
And very dear
Tears trickle down my cheeks
As I see you
Moulder and crumble away
In your coffin
But when I look at the stars
I see you smiling back at me.

Reem Abdulmagied (11)
Katesgrove Primary School, Reading

Smile

Smile
When you're downhearted,
And when you cry,
Don't believe what went by,
Think about the good and forget the bad,
Because your face will emerge with a smile,
And you will show your bright white teeth to the world!

Carry on, carry on,
Laughing all the way,
If your friends are being rude,
Don't change your mood,
Just laugh,
Don't give up, as I'll be there,
Laugh and giggle,
As you only live once,
But if you feel sad,
Just don't forget,
That I'll be there,
To make you smile.

Shubham Kulkarni (11)
Katesgrove Primary School, Reading

The Future

Every day . . . we think about the future,
How will it be many aeons later?
Will we have discovered some new planets called
Lily and Ben?
Will another world war start between you and me?
Will there be robots helping us to work named
Dot and Bot?
Will we live like God, always kind and helpful?
Will we even live?

Everybody knows we cannot answer
those questions now.
So, stop worrying about the future and start to
learn to live
Because . . . it only comes once.

Mehar Bhatia (11)
Katesgrove Primary School, Reading

Love Around Us

There was a girl, her name was Chloe.
Her birthday was soon
And Valentine's Day was in three nights
Would she get a card?
Her birthday passed in a flash
And Valentine's Day was here!
She got a note
Chloe was so happy she shouted
Yippee!

Sinead Kennedy
Kilmodan Primary School, Colintraive

POETRY EMOTIONS - The Joys Of Life

The Sound Of Happiness

I walked to a bright light shining on a button
I pressed it gently but it didn't work
I pressed it again but the same as first
'What's going on?' I said
So I pressed and pressed with all my might
And suddenly let out a squeal of fright
Colours were dancing all over the room
And then I suddenly heard a *zoom!*
A door opened and I heard a sound - a happy, musical sound
I darted forward like a bullet to the door
I swiped at the handle and suddenly heard a roar
Music was ringing in my ears
Happy music was growing louder and louder
I felt the rhythm and tapped my feet
To the sound of the fantastic beat
I was dancing along to an epic song
But suddenly
Everything went white and I stared at the wall
I realised that it was all a happy dream.

Hugo Charles Leigh (8)
Kilmodan Primary School, Colintraive

Happy And Sad

H appy is the best emotion in the world
A nd makes me feel ecstatic
P laces are very exciting
P owerful feeling. Makes you feel like you're gonna shout
Y ippee!

A very lovely feeling and a very
N ice feeling. Makes you feel like you're in a
D aydream

S orry
A nd a powerless feeling
D irty rotten feeling.

Jadelouise Madeline Robertson (8)
Kilmodan Primary School, Colintraive

Competition Time

H ighland dancing makes me happy
I t's my favourite hobby
G eorgina the teacher is the best
H elping us with our steps
L acing our shoes
A nd fixing our hair
N ow it's time to dance
D reaming of winning the trophy

D ancing my way to victory
A ll the team clap
N ow butterflies dance in my tummy
C hildren chant my name
I 'm on top of the world
N ever felt so proud
G rowing up with so many great friends and memories.

Anna Campbell
Newbuildings Primary School, Londonderry

Fear

Fears can be scary, running around in my head
As I lie awake in the dark of the night
Wrapped up in my bed
It's dark outside and wintery
The dogs bark in the park
The wind is howling like a wolf
I'm lying still; eyes closed tight
Scared I'm going to get a fright

I drift to sleep and dream a dream
Of eating lovely nice ice cream
Plus playing football with my team
Bleeping I now hear in my ears
All are gone, my thoughts and fears
The sun is bright in the morning light
I now know things will be all right.

George Guy
Newbuildings Primary School, Londonderry

When I Feel Blue

When I feel blue,
What I like to do,
Is play a little football,
For an hour or two.

That cheers me up,
Playing for my team,
With Adam and Reece,
We are living the dream.

It makes me tired,
But I'm not sad anymore,
Mum's run me a bath,
Bubbles galore!

Dayne Roberts
Newbuildings Primary School, Londonderry

I Am So Hungry

Apple, orange, mmm, so good, all I want is food
Cabbage stew, all I want is you
Want to go to the shop but no money and it's
not so sunny
My friend has food, mmm, so good, someone has food, is it Buddy?
I wish I had food, so good I want a chippy but
it's so nippy
I've got the cold, not so good, all I want is food
Mum said she was buying treats, so I went for a walk in the street
Rang my mum in a queue but home in a few
Carrots, bananas, mmm, so good, does anyone else like food?
Pear, grapes, mmm, so good, but only if I could
Mum got home, till ran out of order.
So hungry, haven't even got a quarter.
No food for me, not so good!

Rebekah Loughlin (10)
Newbuildings Primary School, Londonderry

Is It Time . . .?

I feel a rumbling in my tummy,
that can only mean one thing.

Watching the clock,
time goes so slow,
I wish I'd eaten my breakfast now.

Finally I hear the bell ring for lunch,
so off I go prepared to munch.

Oh no, I hope there isn't a queue,
to my relief there's only a few.

I munch and I crunch as I eat my lunch,
yum, yum, it's time for lunch!

Ella Hughes (10)
Newbuildings Primary School, Londonderry

POETRY EMOTIONS - The Joys Of Life

Love Is Good

L ove is like walking on air
O thers think it's like cuddling a bear
V aluable time spent together
E ven in all types of weather

I ce cream shared on summer days
S unny afternoons, relaxing on sandy bays

G randparents and grandchildren playing on green grass
O thers screaming loudly and having a blast
O pening presents they bought, just shrieked, 'Love!'
D esperately happy as a turtle dove!

Ellie Byron
Newbuildings Primary School, Londonderry

My Birthday

On my birthday I had lots of fun
Me and my friends went to the cinema with my mum
All the presents I got were lovely!
On that day I was really bubbly
In the cinema we watched 'Snoopy and Charlie Brown'
On my cake was a pink and white crown
In the cinema I sat beside my mum
Then we went to McDonald's to fill my tum
Now I am ten
Then I got a new pen.

Abbie Thompson
Newbuildings Primary School, Londonderry

Highland Dancing In Blackpool

B rave at heart
L ight on feet
A ll take to the stage
C ostumes glitter in the ballroom
K icking our legs high
P retending not to be nervous
O verwhelmed with the support of parents
O ver the moon with our dance
L ike we are superstars on TV.

Alex Campbell
Newbuildings Primary School, Londonderry

Happiness

When you go on holidays you're happy
You're active and never snappy
You think of the sun, ice cream and seaside
And your family by your side
You go playing in a park
As big as Noah's ark
Playing with your friends
the fun will never end.

Rachel Watson
Newbuildings Primary School, Londonderry

POETRY EMOTIONS - The Joys Of Life

My Birthday

I woke up with a big smile on my face
I ran down the stairs like I was in a race
I opened my presents with my mum and dad
I was overjoyed with the presents that I had
I got a pug T-shirt
I like to wear it with my black skirt
My nan gave me a new backpack
It was a colourful sack
I went out for a meal on my birthday
I hope everything goes my own way
I had a beef burger, it was nice
I'm glad it wasn't served with rice
After the meal I had ice cream
It was so big I wanted to scream
Then we went home in the car
It was very far
And that was my birthday.

Ella Leanne Phillips (9)
Oak Field Primary School, Barry

A Happy Day

The sun is shining in my room,
Me thinking of my friends, ready to
play with my friends,
I woke my parents up and asked if I can go out,
They said yes!

I went out and played football over the park on this beautiful sunny day,
I was on my friend's team,
The score was six all,
It was time to go home,
I had my tea, had a bath and went to bed,
I went to bed because of school.

Charleigh-Kate Wheatley (11)
Oak Field Primary School, Barry

Love And Friendship

Love can make you happy
Or the person you're in love with can make you happy
Friends can help you or play
Out or in school you can see many friends
Play together every day and hope friendship
never will go away

Both of them can be important
Love and friendship together can make you live a forever-happy life

Love for all of them, so then they mix
So I choose love and friendship
Because they're important to me!

Leo Phillips (10)
Oak Field Primary School, Barry

Sadness

S ad as sad can be because my sister hurt me
A nd called me names like 'Zombie Brains'
D efend myself I did, I kicked her leg
N ot that I should have
E very day it happens I feel sad after school
S o now every day is droopy
S ometimes it's not the same, sometimes I sadly sit in sadness.

Gabriella Robson
Oak Field Primary School, Barry

Anger Is Horrid

A nger is angry
N aughty anger
G reetings, anger
E very day I am angry with my brother
R eally angry with my mum

Anger smells horrid
Anger is as hot as a volcano.

Malachi Mattraves (8)
Oak Field Primary School, Barry

A Happy Day Ahead

Wake up in the morning feeling happy
It's a marvellous day ahead while the sun is shining
With a big smile on my face and a sweety taste
in my mouth
My face is glowing when I see my presents
My best friends come over to play on my birthday
It was a great day today.

Brooke Leigh Seer (10)
Oak Field Primary School, Barry

Movie Night Time

I feel this when I eat popcorn
And when I'm cosy under the blanket
When it's movie night I always have this feeling
When my mum gives me hugs
There is no better feeling
What feeling am I?

Chantelle Wheatley
Oak Field Primary School, Barry

Happiness

Chocolate is the best
It has the best taste
Everyone eats the rest
Try not to waste
Chocolate makes me happy
So I am not snappy.

Kairan Cummins-Free (8)
Oak Field Primary School, Barry

Anger Bubbling Inside

A nger is a fiery bull
N oisy as an erupting volcano
G rowling noises coming from inside
E motions confused, don't know whether to shout or cry
R age takes over, starts to be sly, words and objects flying through the sky.

Ellis Miller (8)
Oak Field Primary School, Barry

Happy Day

Today will be a happy day
Wake up, make your bed, hooray for today!
Joy is an emotion that makes you feel great
You can pass this onto a friend or a mate
This makes you calm and fills you with pride
Inside you feel like you could fly.

Maddison Brady
Oak Field Primary School, Barry

Anger

Anger is dark blood-red
It tastes like spicy salsa that burns the flesh
on your tongue
It is a jalapeño pepper terrorising your mouth
as you bite down
It smells like smoke burning from a house fire
It is fireworks crackling in the air
It looks like a path of dead flowers
It is clenching fists pounding on your door
It sounds like screams of pain
It is bombs going off
Anger is fierce.

Kadee Leigh Williams
Plasnewydd Primary School, Maesteg

Excitement

Excitement is bouncing baby pink
It tastes like scrumptious sticky toffee pudding
It is a bag of colourful fresh candy
It smells like new morning's clear air
Excitement is clean clothes gleaming
with strawberry scent
Like a room of budding bright daisies
It is a thousand smiles spread across every face
Excitement is like the sound of a
spontaneous singing choir
It is screaming joyful children on Christmas Day
Excitement makes the sun come out.

Lucy Marie Davies (11)
Plasnewydd Primary School, Maesteg

Happiness

Happiness is bright yellow
Happiness is like the sun
It tastes like chips at the seaside
It is a beach BBQ
It smells like strong vinegar
It is a Sunday roast
It is velvet on a cloak
It's like a tropical paradise
Happiness is the sound of children in the park
Like people having a great time
Happiness puts a spring in my step.

Ethan Lloyd Morris (11)
Plasnewydd Primary School, Maesteg

Anger

Anger is dark red, like blood
Tasting like super sour sweets sizzling on my tongue
Anger is red-hot chillies setting fire to my mouth
Smelling like a burning fire in the woods
Anger chokes me like car fumes
Like something deep down appearing from
the darkness
Anger looks intimidating to me
Sounds as if you're snapping
Anger sounds like a tree whistling in the wind
Anger scares me.

Lucie Daniel (10)
Plasnewydd Primary School, Maesteg

Fear

Fear is as purple as a violet flower
It tastes like gone-off broccoli
It is a fresh human bone
It smells like a rotten egg from a garbage bin
It is the smell of smoke burning from a house
It looks like a dark grey cloud following you in the sky
It is a child getting bullied in the street
It is the sound of slow footsteps in the
back of your head
It is the sound of a soul shouting, 'Help!' out of a burning house
Fear scares me.

Rebecca Leigh Jones (10)
Plasnewydd Primary School, Maesteg

Fear

Fear is black like the dark alleyway in your head
It tastes like the sour saliva when you're traumatised
It is rotting cereal trapped in your mouth
It smells like stale milk mounted to the fridge
for a decade
It is the scent of millions of dead flowers
It looks like a fiery demon of hatred
It is a dark memory of the past
Fear sounds like the burning of others
It is a frightened scream
Fear intimidates me, fear frightens me.

Ethan Saxby
Plasnewydd Primary School, Maesteg

Happiness

Happiness is sunshine-yellow
Happiness tastes like lush Skittles
It smells like a luscious summer breeze
Happiness looks like Wales singing in the rain
Like birds chirping on a summer day
Happiness sounds like children playing
in the playground
Happiness is having a laugh with your friends
Happiness feels like doing things you love
Happiness puts a smile on my face.

Harvey Ellis Williams
Plasnewydd Primary School, Maesteg

Sadness

Sadness is dull, dark and grey
It tastes like mouldy old cheese
Sadness is a piece of soggy bread
It smells like drenched bathers
Sadness is a goth who smells of sweat
Sadness looks like a family at a funeral
It is a lonely boy by himself in the playground
Sadness sounds like a young boy weeping
It is the sound of adults arguing
Sadness feels like losing someone you love.

Sam Powell
Plasnewydd Primary School, Maesteg

Crazy

Crazy is a sour apple
Crazy is green as grass
It's lovely, luscious lemons
It tastes like multicoloured Skittles
Crazy smells like home-made cookies
It looks like dancing daisies
It sounds like Katie's laughter
Crazy is funny!
It makes you laugh out loud
Crazy makes a cuckoo clock look silly.

Lily May Lavercombe (11)
Plasnewydd Primary School, Maesteg

Fear

Fear is a black shadow in the distance
It tastes like mouldy rice pudding left on a table
It's cold, icy, cold tea
Fear smells like gone off broccoli
Like steam coming out of a chimney
Fear is when you're alone but
someone is watching you
Fear is when you're never safe
It is when you can't get away from yourself
You will never be alone.

Lola Olivia Videan (11)
Plasnewydd Primary School, Maesteg

Anger

Anger is red and hot
It tastes like the hottest chillies ever
It is sour sweets tingling in my mouth
It smells like a big blazing fire
It is crackling fireworks bursting in the air
It looks like crocodiles snapping at each other
It is people arguing fiercely
Sounds like army planes whizzing by
It is fierce fighters fighting
Anger makes me feel out of control.

Katie Louise Thomas (10)
Plasnewydd Primary School, Maesteg

Happiness

Happiness is sunshine-yellow
Happiness tastes like ice cream on a sunny day
It is chunky chips on a bench at the beach
It smells like vinegar on your chips
It is a BBQ on a hot summer's day
Happiness looks like children playing in the park
It is a magical kingdom in a far-off land
Happiness sounds like people laughing
It is wrapping paper ripping on Christmas morning
Happiness makes me feel invincible!

Ethan Morgan Seymour (11)
Plasnewydd Primary School, Maesteg

POETRY EMOTIONS - The Joys Of Life

Happiness

Happiness is bright yellow
It tastes like lovely lemons
It is chocolate on a Christmas morning
It smells like delicious chips on the beach
It is a field of lovely flowers
It looks like the sunset at night
It is little children playing
It sounds like young children laughing
It is carols in a Christmas concert
Happiness brings a huge smile on my face.

Hayden Smith
Plasnewydd Primary School, Maesteg

Sadness

Sadness is the blue on a rainbow
It tastes like cold and mouldy chicken
It is dry porridge from a wicked woman
It smells like a dead rat down the sewers
It is old, rotten cabbage soup
It looks like a lonely child in the pouring rain
It is a homeless man on the street
It sounds like the rain drumming on your house
It is a tornado appearing in the sky
Sadness is a lonely feeling taking over your mind.

Macie Freeman
Plasnewydd Primary School, Maesteg

Excited

Excitement is a bright, colourful rainbow
It tastes like sour sweets sizzling in your mouth
It is a warm chocolate-coated cake
It smells like strong salted popcorn
It is the sweet smell of strawberry candyfloss
It looks like a meadow of dancing daisies
Excitement is a hot summer's day
It sounds like children screaming with excitement
It is the music of a funfair nearby
It feels like joy bursting in the air.

India Williams
Plasnewydd Primary School, Maesteg

Hate

Hate is red, angry and grey
It tastes like hot chilli pepper
It is a spicy taco crunching in your mouth
It smells like the steam off a train
It is in the sewers down in London
Hate is like an abandoned house
Hate is a red hot volcano about to explode
Sounds like shouting downstairs
It is screaming at the top of your lungs
Hate feels like horror.

Ellie Mullins
Plasnewydd Primary School, Maesteg

POETRY EMOTIONS - The Joys Of Life

Love

Love is poppy red
It is lovely, luscious lemons
It tastes like a beautiful dinner
Love smells like happy Valentine's Day
It looks like a rainbow on a hot summer's day
Love is a happy movie in the cinema
It sounds like Only Boys Aloud singing in a concert
It is wedding bells ringing in my ears
Love makes me fresh forever.

Nieve Keddy
Plasnewydd Primary School, Maesteg

Happiness

Happiness is rhubarb-red,
It tastes like super sour sweets,
It is lovely lemon liquorice,
It smells like horrific hot dogs,
It is ridiculously reeking rainbow drops,
It looks like Prince William waving,
It sounds like Wales fans singing,
It is happy children hopping,
Happiness puts pride in my country.

Casey White
Plasnewydd Primary School, Maesteg

Sadness

Sadness is as blue as the sea
The taste of melted ice cubes in your mouth
Smells like dirty, damp dog
It's like being locked in a room with the darkness
It's like swimming in a river of tears
The sound of unknown children
It is a whisper from the dark side
It's the miserable feeling inside you
Sadness corrupts me.

Natisha Blower
Plasnewydd Primary School, Maesteg

Sadness

Sadness is a dark ocean blue
It tastes like salty water that no one wants to drink
It's a sour lemon bursting on you're taste buds
It smells like damp coming from the wall
And moss falling from the ceiling
It sounds like people crying in the corner
People screaming in horror
Sadness makes me feel miserable and lonely.

Ffion Rumph (11)
Plasnewydd Primary School, Maesteg

Hate

Hate is as grey as a foggy sky
It is your worst nightmare coming to your town
Hate is as hot as smoking lava
It is hot peppers burning your soul
Hate smells like gas getting closer to you
It's fire damaging everything
Hate looks like a dark alleyway getting colder
Hate frustrates me!

Olivia Castle
Plasnewydd Primary School, Maesteg

Untitled

Love is beautiful bright pink
It tastes like super sweet strawberries
It smells like a field of fantastic flowers
Love is a dancing dandelion
The sound of love is a bunch of children
cheering in joy
Love brightens my heart.

Charlie Acteson
Plasnewydd Primary School, Maesteg

Oh, Fear!

Oh, Fear!
Don't be afraid of a deer,
Anyway, it's not that near,
So don't be afraid of a deer!

Oh, Fear!
Don't be afraid of a smear,
Anyway, we can clean it up clear,
So don't be afraid of a smear!

Oh, Fear!
Don't be afraid of Lincolnshire,
Anyway, we're staying here,
So don't be afraid of Lincolnshire!

Oh, Fear!
Don't be afraid of the next school year,
Anyway, the kids won't jeer,
So don't be afraid of the next school year!

Leah Grevatt (10)
Platt CE Primary School, Sevenoaks

Worried

It was a dark, dull day,
I was worried and alone,
I didn't have my playmate,
George was on his own.

His cheeks were pale clouds,
As he lay there, a still stone,
I tried to cheer him up
With an ice cream cone!

He'd been ill for ages,
I could stand it no more!
We'd been on a cruise six days
And he'd been sick for half the tour.

When George started to recover,
Worries turned to joy!
Finally, himself again,
Such a lovely boy!

Bryer Icela Zagas Lowe (7)
Platt CE Primary School, Sevenoaks

A Beautiful Place

It's kinda strange the way I'm feeling today
There's something I just can't disguise
It may not seem a lot to you, but if I found a way
I'd take us to an island where we both could be free
If I could paint a picture for you
Or write a leading role in Broadway show
It may not seem that much, but I offer to you
I write these words so I can let you know that this is from the heart . . .

I went out for a walk through the park
And thought about the picture I was painting for you
Since the rain has stopped falling down
I can feel the brush strokes flowing from my hand
But there's nobody other than you
who can really understand
So don't take this so badly cos it's what I have to do
I can't seem to remember the day I first saw you
but all that really matters is that you've become the sweetest thing my eyes have ever seen.

You can keep it to yourself, or you can tell the world
There seems no reason to hold it inside
So let's sing it out
I want to sing it out loud
We can shout it from the rooftops
Let it rain down on the crowd!

You make the world a beautiful place . . .

You make the world a beautiful place.

Georgia Ellen Stronge (15)
Stepping Stones School, Hindhead

POETRY EMOTIONS - The Joys Of Life

Toy Soldiers

Wild winds blow against my scarred skin.
Cruel November has left its mark on No-Man's-Land.
A single bird lands on the muddy road ahead; it's the red-breasted robin.
Looking around me, I see the damage by the wrath of God's hand.
I see them, piled up on top of each other
Toy soldiers.

Battered and bruised. None of them look asleep.
I still hear the last cry as they run into the firing lines.
I think of families miles away who weep.
For those brave men who now by the road lie,
As if they were just knocked over, flippantly, by a little boy at play.
Toy soldiers.

My stomach growls at me, angry because it hasn't been fed.
The scent of sulphur and mud scream together in the freezing air.

My vision is suddenly stained red
The bomb goes off underfoot, and I fall into
the hard earth.
And you still stand there, telling me war is best for all?
You are wrong, through and through.
Never be drawn, if your hear No-Man's-Land call
You don't know, you'll never know how many of the brave will fall.
Toy soldiers.

Hannah (Bo) Longley
Stepping Stones School, Hindhead

The Blooming World

The tear rolled down her chiselled cheek
Her eyes swelled with magic
Her heart beat with fright
Her face fell with the sight
Like the sea had washed her up
She saw the light; her tears dried up

Her heart stopped. She lay there still
In the blooming world
Daring to step further, one step on
Daring to be other than who she was
Daring to become the impossible,
to be the achievable.
Never again would she say no to her own life.
On she would go
On she would soar
Into the living land she would stand.

Jade Lily Mansell (15)
Stepping Stones School, Hindhead

To Ness

No one is really gone,
They still live on through us
If we keep on telling stories about them.
Everywhere they went; every word they said.
Every year of every month, of every week of every
day of every hour of every minute of every second
you spent with them.
I write this in loving memory
of Ness.
A funny, caring woman.
She will always be with all of us.
Don't stop remembering.

Lucas Harman
Stepping Stones School, Hindhead

POETRY EMOTIONS - The Joys Of Life

Happiness

Happiness can appear
Whether you're far from home or near
When happiness is here
I start to smile from ear to ear

Some people have all the money in the world
Yet their only wish is collecting all the money which is at them hurled

Some people have nothing but the clothes on
their bodies
Yet they are as happy and calm as a
warm summer breeze

How is it possible for people in this situation to be so wrapped up with happiness?
This is because being happy with what you have is the true source of happiness.

Yisrolik Itzinger (10)
Talmud Torah Tiferes Shlomoh, London

Surprise Birthday Party

One day I came home from school,
everything was dark.
'What happened? Was there a blackout?' I did remark.
The lights turned on. 'Happy birthday,'
everyone did say.
And boy did I forget it was my birthday today.
Balloons and streamers were all over the room.
Wow was I happy, I wanted to climb to the moon.
Cakes and cookies, all of the treats I love and like.
And for my birthday present I got a brand-new bike.
'Thank you Mum and Dad for my wonderful birthday.
I can't wait for my birthday next year,' I will say.

Refoel Duvid Weitz (11)
Talmud Torah Tiferes Shlomoh, London

The Great Day

Today is my birthday,
As happy as they say,
Presents are flowing,
Take them I am going,
I look so great,
So said my friend Nate,
We danced until night,
Then came dawn light,
We are so happy,
Until our voices were raspy,
It was time to go home,
Home, sweet home!

Moishy Fierstone
Talmud Torah Tiferes Shlomoh, London

Switzerland

S weating on the high mountains
W ow, such beautiful waterfalls running down
I love going on walks and outings
T o go on cable cars up and down
Z oos and parks we go to
E veryone is excited and happy
R ivers and waters
L unch has arrived after a full day of walking down
A ll of us go and take a rest
N ever had such fun
D eparting was the hardest part.

Boruch Freshwater
Talmud Torah Tiferes Shlomoh, London

POETRY EMOTIONS - The Joys Of Life

Canada

C ool in the summer
A nd frozen in the winter
N iagara Falls flowing down
A t schools people are going everywhere
D ay after day it's getting nicer
A lso have lots of ice skating.

Shmelky Pinter (10)
Talmud Torah Tiferes Shlomoh, London

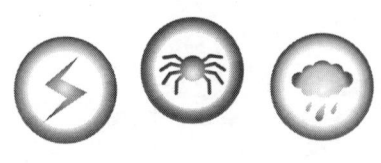

Young Writers Information

We hope you have enjoyed reading this book – and that you will continue to in the coming years.

If you're a young writer who enjoys reading and creative writing, or the parent of an enthusiastic poet or story writer, do visit our website www.youngwriters.co.uk. Here you will find free competitions, workshops and games, as well as recommended reads, a poetry glossary and our blog.

If you would like to order further copies of this book, or any of our other titles, then please give us a call or visit **www.youngwriters.co.uk**.

Young Writers
Remus House
Coltsfoot Drive
Peterborough
PE2 9BF
(01733) 890066 / 898110
info@youngwriters.co.uk